ORDINARY PEOPLE

ORDINARY PEOPLE

Family Life and Global Values

MICHAEL TRUE

ORBIS BOOKS

Maryknoll, New York 10545

The Catholic Foreign Mission Society of America (Maryknoll) recruits and trains people for overseas missionary service. Through Orbis Books, Maryknoll aims to foster the international dialogue that is essential to mission. The books published, however, reflect the opinions of their authors and are not meant to represent the official position of the society.

Library of Congress Cataloging-in-Publication Data

True, Michael.
    Ordinary people: family life and global values / Michael True.
      p. cm.
    Includes bibliographical references.
    ISBN 0-88344-738-X
    1. Social justice—Study and teaching—United States. 2. Peace—
Study and teaching—United States. 3. Values—Study and teaching—
United States. 4. Parenting—United States. 5. Parenting—
Religious aspects—Christianity. I. Title.
HM216.T782   1991
649′.1—dc20   90-22590
                                              CIP

for
Jonathan
Juliann
Shannon
Laurel
Daniel
Alison

THE FUTURE: It's our life, and our children's and our grandchildren's. What will it be like?

—Mary E. Clark
Ariadne's Thread

People whose integrity has not been damaged in childhood, who were protected, respected, and treated with honesty by their parents, . . . will take pleasure in life and will not feel any need to kill or even hurt others or themselves. . . . It will be inconceivable to such people that earlier generations had to build up a gigantic war industry in order to feel comfortable and safe in the world.

—Alice Miller
For Your Own Good

Teach your children what we have taught our children, that the Earth is our mother.

—Chief Seattle

CONTENTS

Part III
AUTHENTIC WAYS OF DOING

Part IV
CONCLUSION

PREFACE

This is a book about teaching values in the midst of social change. Its focus is the home, where patterns are learned and where children face the choices and conflicts of later life for the first time. Writing out of the experience of family life, I try to make sense of particular tasks associated with rearing children in a nuclear age, in an imperial culture. My emphasis is upon values that not only shape but also help to sustain family life, particularly those that recognize the interdependency between people and the world around them.

Like many parents, I am concerned about how we and our progeny might live as responsible "citizens of the world" (William Lloyd Garrison's noble phrase) in a culture that is increasingly competitive, violent, and careless about the future. As a father and grandfather, I take seriously events in recent history that have altered the context within which parents teach and children learn what they believe to be good.

This book, informed by further reading and reflection and ten additional years of experience in parenting, is, in some ways, a sequel to an earlier discussion of the subject. During the time I wrote *Homemade Social Justice* (1982), our children were fifteen to twenty-two years of age; now they are twenty-five to thirty-two. Then we were a family of eight; now we are a community of seventeen—daughters-in-law, son-in-law, and grandchildren included.

In the recent decades, the culture of the United States has been substantially altered. The poverty rate has increased by one-third, and the income of young families has declined by 25 percent. Today, people in the lower 40 percent of the economy receive less than 16 percent of the nation's total income, the lowest share on record in U.S. history. The Reagan administration alone cut funding for education by one-quarter and tripled the national debt.

Other presidents and legislators, with the support of many voters, have systematically dismantled social and educational services, many of them established and strengthened over a fifty-year period. In spite of an almost unchallenged military build-up, the country never appeared more vulnerable.

Many psychologists, ethicists, and others with similar concerns argue that we simply do not meet basic needs associated with growth and development in various stages of life, such as a commitment to community and the next generation. The consequences of this neglect have been deeply disruptive at every level, making many Americans more anxious and more uncertain about the meaning of life and prospects for the future. A significant number of people expect large-scale nuclear devastation within twenty years.

Not surprisingly, many students in American schools and colleges have indicated, "on the one hand, that their lives are likely to end in a nuclear war and, on the other hand, that there is no point in worrying about it since it is bound to happen anyway," as Freeman Dyson has said. Some young people, including many of the most talented among them, turn to drugs and even to suicide as a way out, choosing death, or some spiritual or psychological approximation of it, as the only relief from increasingly painful lives.

That's the bad news. The good news is that, daily, increasing numbers of people risk their lives and fortunes to stop the arms race, to alleviate human suffering, and to build a new social order. Elizabeth McAlister, for example, impeded the shipment of nuclear missiles to Europe from Griffiss (New York) Air Force Base (and sacrificed three years in Alderson Federal Prison as a result of it). Helen Woodson and Carl Kabat, O.M.I., dismantled nuclear silos in the Midwest (and now endure eight to twelve years behind bars for doing so). Meanwhile, Veterans for Peace defied Reagan's economic boycott of Nicaragua by transporting food and medicine to the people of that beleaguered country, and Charlie Litecky and Bill Perry, "breaking ranks," left the military and the defense industry to join the peace movement.

Others work daily in the shadow of the White House and across the country, performing traditional works of mercy: feeding the hungry, housing the homeless, comforting the sick, counseling the sorrowful; and resourceful social workers and teachers help immigrant peoples become assimilated in a new culture. Elsewhere, small groups, such as the Union of Concerned Scientists, Greenpeace, and Cultural Survival, Inc., organize to prevent disaster by protecting natural resources and endangered peoples.

In the midst of conflicting values, parents must make hard choices about how to live responsibly, including how to help their children make informed decisions about the future. This book, a kind of search for moral norms in a pluralistic society, includes stories about some parents' attempts to face this challenge. Respecting their effort and confusion, their successes and failures, it is addressed to anyone involved in the elemental, essential task of parenting (alone or with others) or to anyone who shares the domestic life of children, from the early years through late adolescence. Recognizing that the care and nurturing of human beings, the rightful task of any humane culture, begins in the home, I mention—tentatively, conservatively— ways of proceeding: some elementary "suggestions for the long haul," at the end of chapter 1, for example, and reflections on the relationship between values in the home and in the wider community, in the private and the public spheres.

In making suggestions, I am aware always of the tentative nature of parenting, including my own failure to teach the values I recommend. This latter fact was brought home to me recently as a young Catholic Worker and I watched his son and my grandson—both four years old—chasing one another through our kitchen and dining room "shooting" one another with "rifles" imagined out of two old hockey sticks they had found in our basement. The boys were having the time of their lives playing war games, as their pacifist elders stood, a bit bemused, recognizing that something had gone wrong, somewhere. One teaches social justice as one teaches any other system of values to children, knowing that the results may be mixed at best.

Becoming a "citizen of the world" is a long-term process, related to ways of maintaining and transforming the self. Its proper grounding is a sense of continuity between past and present, and of worldwide interconnectedness. As a man, I have had a hard time learning about interdependence, in personal as well as public life. In struggle and perhaps in defeat, I began to recognize my unconscious acceptance of an individualistic ethic of "going it alone," and began to consider alternatives. How might we live in such a way as to recognize our dependence upon others and our interconnectedness to all living things? And how might we teach our children to honor similar values? Institutions—church, school, and government—occasionally help in this effort, but are likely to do so only if parents and children initiate it.

Although this book makes certain assumptions about what life is for and how it might be lived, I recommend these values without ignoring the complex issues involved or the context in which we try to live them. My perspective is—broadly speaking—religious, with a deep respect for the feelings, beliefs, and practices associated with all peoples' attempts to understand "the meaning of life," including explanations available to us from European and North American culture. I take seriously powerful new ideas associated with liberation theology and the cries of the poor in Latin America, Asia, and Africa, as well as insights about "the myth" of Christian uniqueness, provided by religious scholars in the United States and Europe.

An implicit theme throughout is that when we accommodate traditions previously ignored or slighted by the institutional church we often begin to think about religion more attentively than we have in the past, and perhaps begin to redefine the word. (Living in China for extended periods since 1984 has undoubtedly influenced my perspective here.) The fact that our children are sometimes "religious" in ways quite different from our own is one of the many complications in teaching moral values.

But why "ordinary people"? Because in the work or vocation of parenting, every one of us is "ordinary" in this sense: we want for our own and for all children the common necessities—food, clothing, shelter, "clean air, green grass, not being pushed around," as Paul Goodman once said. We want them to enjoy a long and happy life, in the midst of some of the good things we have enjoyed—basic human rights and some material comfort. Yes, by the standards of a world in which a third of the children go to bed hungry every night, such expectations are "extraordinary." But for much of the population, some of these necessities are or could be available, so our expectations for our children are not unreasonable.

And we are "ordinary" in another sense as well, being vulnerable and often at the mercy of people in power who ignore the harmful effects of militarism and imperialism, political repression and economic oppression. "Children," as Daniel Berrigan has said, "are a pledge that something other than a wantonly wrecked creation is our legacy." Unless, as parents, we uphold the sacredness of the earth and the importance of "ordinary people," we—and our children—simply may not survive.

"We're bound to each other with unknown thread," the Polish poet Piotr Summer has written, "a stitch of red corpuscles sewing up the globe." Understanding interdependence is not a simple matter; communicating it to children takes conscious effort—imagination, patience, and (most of all) love. To have a concern for others, says the moral psychologist Tom Kitwood, is "to experience a feeling, a 'movement of the soul,' " in which those others are honored and respected as if they were oneself. In the following discussion, I regard this concept as essential to parenting and offer a few hints about passing it along.

This book, like the earlier one, was written "in the middle of things," as our children grow into adulthood and our grandchildren begin to make their way in the world. Each day has tested what was written the day before, limiting the danger of the discussion's becoming merely academic, I hope.

In sounding an alert about the world our children are moving into, I concentrate on the difficulties, rather than the joys, of child-rearing. Acknowledging difficulties frees up energy for recognizing pleasures, as Carol Bly has suggested, adding that it is no accident "that the most openly praising and enthusiastic writers are those who do not pass off evil as 'the way it goes, I guess.' " My recognizing the difficulties of parenting is one way of praising that vocation; treating it seriously is another.

Our responsibility to become "citizens of the world" and to

live in friendship with the earth must somehow be reduced to the scale of our competence as parents. In the following "essay" or "attempt," I try to provide a rationale, with suggestions, for doing just that.

Acknowledgments

I am grateful to Salve Regina College for the opportunity to explore aspects of this discussion, in the Atwood Lectures, and to various people who provided information and commentary: Suzanne Belote and Brayton Shanley, Bea Charette, Brien Connolly, Kathy and Bob Fry, Holly Griffin, Kathleen and Jim Jolin, Chris Kiernan, Mark McCarthy, Nancy McBride, Carol Proietti, S.S.A., Scott and Claire Schaeffer-Duffy, David Senecal, and Chuck Stewart. Liza Bliss, Alfreda Altobelli, Anna Kung, and Lynne Robbins recommended children's books related to the theme of this book. For many fruitful discussions about peace studies, I am grateful to Maryanne Guertin, S.S.J., Brian Keaney, Werner Brion, Meg Brodhead, and Glen Gersmehl, who provided the marvelous quote from Ennio Flaiano—as well as to the Center for International Cooperation and Security Studies, University of Wisconsin, Madison, whose summer seminar I participated in while thinking about this book.

Hank Schlau's story about meeting a young father on a train who wanted help in teaching his children about social justice set me to writing initially. Paul Giaimo, Carol Bly, Tim Heffernan, and Stephen and Nancy True made valuable criticisms at a crucial point, calling me to account and making this a better book than it might have been. Parents too numerous to mention contributed stories and useful reflections. Without the encouragement of all of these people—and support, early on, from Richard Oehling, Assumption College—I would have never attempted writing such a book; without their suggestions and criticisms, I would have never completed it.

My indebtedness to writers in various disciplines is indicated by a listing of their works in the bibliography, including several contemporary poets whose work provides extraordinary insight into how Americans think and feel at this moment in history. As with other writers of books, similarly indebted, I hereby absolve the above-mentioned people of any responsibility for what is said in the following pages.

Finally and especially, I benefited from the contributions of Mary Pat True, school psychologist, editor, and grandmother to the six young people named in the dedication.

PART I

TEACHING VALUES

1

THE TASK

Love, death, the cruelty of power, and time's curve beyond
the stars are what children want to look at.
— Carol Bly
"Growing Up Expressive"

Attentive mothers or fathers learn very early that child-rearing is fraught with unexpected difficulties. The task — even after
one survives the initial responsibilities of feeding, diapering, and
nurturing — resembles a walk through an obstacle course, with
parents never knowing what sand trap, water hole, or booby trap
awaits them from one moment to the next. So some of us look
for help — suggestions, not lectures — in pirouetting our way
across a tricky landscape. In this, as in other human activities,
as Ennio Flaiano says, "The shortest distance between two
points is the arabesque."

Hard realists, parents are understandably skeptical toward
anyone speaking with assurance about teaching values to children, let alone writing a book on the subject. Yet because moral
education is so important and the times unprecedented, we, in
the day-to-day, moment-by-moment task of parenting, look for
new ways to be thoughtful and purposeful in encouraging our
children to be good.

In writing this book, I kept remembering a story about the
mother of four teenage children who went to a program several
years ago on teaching values to children. She heard a young

3

couple talk enthusiastically about how their children responded to their efforts to teach social justice; how, after studying documents on peace and human rights (from the United Nations and the church), the family incorporated such teachings into their daily lives — at home, work, school. After the lecture, the mother of four walked up to the podium and asked the husband and wife how old their children were. "Six and four," they said cheerfully. "I thought so," the older woman said, as she headed toward the exit.

Thinking of her, I approach the topic of teaching values in the family with caution and modesty. For I am aware that any parent taking the trouble to read further does so half-anxiously, wanting any help he or she can get, and half-skeptically, having been disappointed by similar discussions of this topic too many times before.

Popular writings about many aspects of parenting — for instance, how to care for children physically and psychologically — are often both sophisticated and accessible. Professionals and even journalists, from Dr. Benjamin Spock to Ann Landers, provide sound advice on topics as wide-ranging as diet, medication, discipline, and personal values. Books and women's magazines, as well as the daily newspaper, provide helpful hints about helping children grow into adolescence, handle academic competition, or learn about sexuality. As a veteran parent, I am continually impressed, in fact, not only by the concreteness of these popular writings, but also by the wisdom of the commentators. In moments of panic — as a child's fever soared to 104 degrees or, later, as three young children dropped out of grade school and a teenage daughter refused to attend high school — my wife and I read such articles and books with appreciation and gratitude.

Americans, generally effective problem solvers in other areas of life, are often good parents as well. Watching young married couples juggle two careers, child care, and undergraduate, graduate, or professional training, I am constantly impressed by their resourcefulness. Like earlier generations of parents, they are remarkably attentive in caring for their progeny, while initiating them into a highly industrial, somewhat frantic modern culture. (Isn't it rather bewildering, in fact, the way we dutifully, deliberately prepare our children, as Ellen Goodman has said, "to lead the exact life that we find so rushed"?)

When they discuss teaching social values to children, professionals and general commentators are much less concrete than they are about teaching personal values, however. Looking for suggestions or guidance on such matters, one must conclude that teaching social ethics to children is difficult in ways that people seldom write about in books.

Most writing about teaching values lacks a sense of immediacy because it ignores the psychological crosscurrents of family life, that is, the context in which issues present themselves in the home. Why do such writings, I sometimes wonder, make teaching values look so simple, while I find it so confusing and exhausting? Is it because "the experts" seldom face the day-to-day, moment-by-moment conflicts associated with teaching children to be good? Or do they simply think too abstractly and give too few examples? I have in mind, particularly, values that relate to the resolution of conflict within and outside the family and to the sustaining of relationships based upon cooperation, justice, and peace.

Maintaining peace at the dinner table or resolving neighborhood conflicts nonviolently sounds relatively simple, in the abstract. But when two older children, both strong personalities, begin arguing over supper, or the bully next door clobbers your youngest child, the complications make any resolution seem difficult indeed. Resolving a family feud or speaking with a difficult neighborhood parent, while trying to restore your child's self-image, requires the skill of a U.N. ambassador. At such moments, generalizations such as "Children should be exposed to conceptual frameworks that juxtapose their own moral reactions against those of others," from a recent textbook on moral education, sound terribly far removed from "the struggle." Where does one go for help?

Most television and motion picture renderings of family scenes at such critical moments give an inaccurate rendering of parents' dilemmas. For example, unlike our progeny, television children seldom ask "Why?" every time they are counseled not to cross a street without looking, or not to point a knife toward themselves when cutting bread, or not to lie. In situation comedies, children's conversations about elemental subjects such as family relationships are often highly sentimental; and sexual love is trivialized—or treated as "cute"—by people of all ages. At the other extreme, moral absolutists counsel a hard line, insisting that "letting the kids know who's boss" solves almost any conflict at home, on the playground, or in school.

THE MORAL CHALLENGES OF CHILDREN

Children often expose the vagueness of older people's (including their parents') presuppositions about young people's attitudes and behavior. And, in matters close to home, we naturally find children's moral challenges to our behavior hard to take. "Do you want to get cancer?" my oldest son asked me repeatedly, before I stopped smoking. Similarly, in responding to their frequent questions about social justice, it's easier to silence children than to explain to them, in fifty words or less, why millions of Americans remain homeless, or why factory managers allow pollution to contaminate the workplace, or why we use harmful pesticides, against the advice of environmentalists, in cleaning the sink or caring for the lawn.

Jean Paul Sartre, hardly a household name among commentators on parenting, once told an interviewer: "It is much easier for a philosopher to explain a new concept to another philosopher than to a child, because the child asks the real questions." As adults, we seldom face moral confrontations in our daily lives, though we constantly give moral advice to our children. We insist upon their eating properly, although we continue to buy processed food with little nutritional value. We decry the lack of funds for public education and social services, while squandering money on clothes, furnishings, and cosmetics that we don't need. We lecture them on the value of life, while surrendering a heavy portion of our income to the Pentagon to build nuclear weapons.

Our sons and daughters often throw into relief opinions and arguments that seemed two-dimensional before our children appeared on the scene. At one point, when four of our six children were teenagers, for example, we discouraged one of our sons from associating with a junior-high classmate, because he used every foul expression imaginable (and, tactlessly, just within earshot), and periodically lifted candy and trinkets from the local supermarket. Two days later, we invited the same class-mate over to supper, since he was the only close friend our son had in that torturous no man's land of early adolescence. Some years later our son told us how much he appreciated our treating his friends with respect, even when we disapproved of their behavior, and it was then that we learned that we had behaved wiser than we knew.

Our multiple responsibilities as parents make it difficult to maintain a consistent viewpoint on social issues, particularly in the family. We are required to love our children, to give them a sense of security and self-regard, as well as to teach them to make distinctions between right and wrong—all of this, of course, in the midst of trying to keep them clothed, healthy, and out of trouble.

In making meaning out of their experience, children rely upon their parents and family to provide a "frame" for events around them, day-by-day. I was struck by this fact recently in watching my four-year-old grandson take in the details and try to under-stand the implications of an accident that took place on the street just below his living room window. There, in the late after-noon, the young boy next door narrowly escaped being run over when he dashed from behind a parked car into a narrow, busy street. The sight of his friend lying near the curb, his leg scraped by a fall to the pavement, brought Jonathan near tears, partly out of sympathy for his friend, partly out of fear for his own safety on the same street.

Deciding how to respond to Jonathan at that moment took some thought, for I wanted him to feel safe, not terrorized, by events outside his home. At the same time, my grandson's empa-thy for his friend was a natural concern to be encouraged in any way possible. Yet I wanted the lesson, about being careful near the street, not to be lost on him either. Clarifying the issues associated with events of this kind, while listening carefully to a child's responses, takes time and energy—all part of the effort to teach values in the midst of the more mundane, exhausting tasks of child care. Knowing that a child may well link an inci-dent from early childhood with complex social situations later on, we try to negotiate among various impulses and values that might help him or her make meaning of experience.

In the early years, parents have less trouble than they do later in maintaining some consistency in point of view about values, since a child's experience is limited and the desire to please parents is strong. Yet even then, one must prepare children for the inevitable break that allows them not only to choose but also to reject parents' values. When he was four years old my grandson made such a move by telling his father that he "hated" basketball, knowing it was his father's favorite sport, and indicated his preference for hockey, instead.

Similarly, a young girl surrounded by books during her early life may dramatize her independence from her parents by refusing to read, while another girl, discouraged from using eye shadow and rouge, may choose to become a teenage vamp simply to provoke her father's ire. How long should one wait before responding to such challenges or voicing one's disapproval? And how can that be done without at the same time making children think your love is dependent upon their claiming your values as their own?

As much as I disapprove of guns and war toys for children, for example, I am not at all certain that complete censorship of them for very young children is the best way of their becoming faithful apostles of nonviolence later on. I had to rethink this aspect of "the task" again recently, at the time of the incident (mentioned in the preface) in which my grandson and his close friend ran through our kitchen and dining room "shooting" one another with "rifles" imagined from hockey sticks. Although they had obviously not been encouraged in such behavior, neither his father nor I was certain about the best time to discourage them from such games, popular among American children at almost any age, particularly among the generations brought up on television and surrounded by plastic tanks, machine guns, and helicopters.

Janet Zandy, a mother who refused to buy war toys for her son, has told how circumstance — actual living — blurs our attempts to draw the line on this and other issues. Having a kind of genius for making weapons out of just about anything, her son devoted much of his artwork to that purpose: "Craft projects of tongue depressors, macaroni, and toothpicks became, alas, guns. . . . This is American culture."

Although children cannot be protected for long from unpleasant circumstances, including violence and injustice, they can be made thoughtful about them, even in the early years. By the age of two, some children already understand the difference between others' needs and feelings and their own, and have begun to respond to others' suffering. Early on, they develop what one psychologist calls "global sympathy," as Carolyn Kizer indicates in a poem called "The Worms":

> This was childhood:
> Walking through the worms
> After a rain,
> Trying not to wound
> Anything alive;
> Most especially
> Not to maim the self
> By any kind of death.

Such sentiments need to be nourished at that young age because before long, the countervalue—doing whatever is possible, including killing the insects on sight—brings a child quickly into the "real world" of choice, in his or her response to others.

At the earlier stage, children can pretty well be counted on to want to please their parents and to go along with family customs and values. By the time they are eight or so, however, they may confront us with our inconsistencies and begin to apply their own sense of justice. At that time and especially during early adolescence, children can become very conformist about social values. They do not want their parents to be "different" because they do not want to be different themselves. Although I did not realize it at the time, the behavior of one of our sons, who wanted us to be *more*, rather than less, materialistic—with a newer car, plusher carpet, and a better-paying job—was characteristic of many boys at twelve or fourteen.

During that period, children develop a strong sense of what is fair or unfair; and indeed, our son's criticism of us, because we did not deliver "the goodies" that some of his contemporaries enjoyed, was a protest against life's unfairness to him, at that age. Fifteen years later, with children of his own, he chided us about our bourgeois values. (His mother and I got the essential point across, in other words, only to have it used against us later. So it goes. . . .)

When our progeny reach late adolescence, teaching values becomes a hundred times more complicated, when sex, drugs, and draft registration make the scene. The years from sixteen to eighteen are, psychologists tell us, the time of greatest development in moral judgment. Helping our offspring through this period—as well as surviving it ourselves—can test the physical, psychological, and spiritual strength of the heartiest parents. A mother of four told, for example, about her frustration in trying to reason with her talented but adventuresome teenage son about remaining in school. In the midst of an argument about his behavior, he accused his mother, still in her midforties, of being senile. Offended by his remark, she nonetheless confessed: "You know, though, in trying to reason with him, I *act* senile."

In an increasingly complex, fast-paced culture, is it any wonder that fathers and mothers are simply undone by that struggle?

The fact that adolescents are a prime target for television advertisers and filmmakers further complicates a parent's task. Since about 1980, "the siren songs of the ad business" have been increasingly directed toward teenagers, with some critics seeing a direct link, for example, between the relentless campaign by beer companies and the increase in alcoholism among young people.

I shall return to this discussion of television in chapter 2, as an example of a parent's dilemma, juggling many tasks at once. But before that, I want to suggest, in very general terms, some ways of understanding the challenges of moral education of children, which is what teaching values is all about.

THE MORAL DEVELOPMENT OF CHILDREN

"Values cannot be taught as such; they can only be assimilated," Norman J. Bull, an English ethicist, has said, emphasizing the theoretical and practical dimensions of teaching values. Learning the difference between right and wrong is a process essentially of exploration by the child, "learning through personal experience and, above all, personal involvement." Children, like audiometers, measure, moment-by-moment, the sound waves in their environment, picking up signals about what is important, what not.

Any thoughtful parent wants, in teaching values, to give the right signals at the right time. Yet so often, we begin the task with only rudimentary skills, usually without thinking seriously about the important task before us, and often with only the example of our own parents to guide us in rearing our own children.

Assistance in the task of teaching values to children is available, however. The purpose of this book, as I mentioned in the preface, is to offer a few suggestions about that, some based upon practical experience and some related to new theoretical writing and research in moral education, from a variety of disciplines. Among the many interdisciplinary approaches to teaching values or moral education, the work of Lawrence Kohlberg is particularly useful in its implications for teaching social values in the family.

Without discussing them at length — or responding to his critics — I do want to describe Kohlberg's theories of moral development. In extensive studies of children in various cultures, particularly Mexico, Taiwan, and the United States, Kohlberg dramatized the close relationship between a child's intellectual and moral development. Some of his observations, which may seem almost self-evident to any attentive mother or father, are useful as reference points to any adult — parent, teacher, boy scout or girl scout leader — involved in teaching global values to children.

Building upon the writings of Jean Piaget and Paul Tillich about how people "learn justice," Kohlberg describes six stages of moral development in children, with attention to their motives for action at each point along the way. According to this theory, a child's ability to reason about moral issues develops from the preconventional or self-oriented level (stages 1 and 2) to the conventional (and transitional) or society-oriented level (stages 3 and 4) and then to the postconventional or principled level (stages 5 and 6).

In stage 1, for example, a child's action is motivated by a wish to avoid punishment or to obey the rules. A two-year-old told "Don't run into the street or I will make you sit in the corner" will usually refrain from doing so. In stage 2 his or her action is motivated by a wish to be rewarded or to be fair. A child might clean up her room, for example, since she knows that her allowance for that week depends upon it, or that it helps her parents as well.

At the next level, a child becomes increasingly concerned with mutuality and interpersonal relationships. In stage 3 action is motivated by a fear of not living up to others' expectations and, therefore, of feeling bad about oneself. A young boy mows the lawn, for example, in order *not* to feel ashamed when his father spends his holiday doing the same task. In school he tries to operate by the Golden Rule. In stage 4 action is motivated out of a dread of harming others: A teenage son shovels the walk, for example, before being asked to do so, in order to prevent family and neighbors from falling on the ice. Or a teenage daughter refrains from driving home drunk from a party, not just from fear of losing her license, but from fear of running into someone else.

At the next level, a child recognizes the benefits to society of human rights or moral values. At stage 5, for example, your son may agree to collect signatures to establish a recycling plant in your town, or you and your children sign up to cook dinner for homeless people at a local shelter. In stage 6 action is taken to prevent violating one's own principles. For example, a parent or a son or daughter who opposes killing pickets the execution of a man found guilty of murder or commits civil disobedience by dismantling a nuclear weapon at an arms manufacturing plant, in order to protect the lives of potential victims.

Children move through these or similar stages of moral development in various ways and at different speeds, depending upon their experience of a moral community and a loving home, where moral questions are discussed. Parents and other adults play a crucial role in aiding or abetting that development, not only by the values they live, but also by their manner of teaching values. In working with adolescents, I am often reminded of the influence of a parent, aunt, cousin, or a junior-high-school teacher on a student's attitude toward social issues, including his or her decision about a job after graduation. Not surprisingly, conversations and events affect young people in ways that mothers, fathers, and other adults never intend, so it is wise to give some thought as to how, as well as to what, one wishes to teach, as Kohlberg and other theorists suggest.

LEARNING AS WE GO

In teaching values, showing is obviously better than telling, and asking the right questions is as important as giving the right answers. Reading to children (or by oneself) is a stronger argument against television than lecturing children from the television lounge chair. Similarly, asking questions of children encourages them to make distinctions and to consider, for themselves, "Is this more valuable than that? Why? Why not?" Teaching values means, first of all, conveying that distinctions matter—that some things are more important than others and that human beings make choices based upon these distinctions. Our children's knowing a young college student—a talented, street-smart athlete—who opened a house of hospitality for homeless people in our city impressed them far more than anything we *said* about the corporal works of mercy (feeding the hungry, housing the homeless). But perhaps having heard the value named beforehand helped them to recognize it being lived.

I mention this incident, remembering all the while my failure regarding specific issues of this kind. As with most fathers, much of my own (and *all* of my wife's) energy went into the elemental tasks of feeding, diapering, and protecting our children from harm. When was there time to encourage our daughter's, then our son's, natural curiosity about the way society works, about "love, death, . . . and time's curve beyond the stars"? Weren't they, after all, simply along for the ride? Besides, I often had "more important things to do," such as earning a living and making a place for myself in the world.

Eventually, however, I found myself having to add the task of teaching values to the other responsibilities, relying unconsciously on my parents' example and on the advice of friends with children slightly older than our own. Since my father never resorted to violent measures in disciplining my brothers and me, I seldom spanked our children—not because I had given the matter serious thought beforehand, but because of "the benevolent father" that I carried around in my psyche. Similarly, since my parents rarely talked politics, I had little sense of what to do about my own children's education in social values.

At a critical point, about 1964, however, history intervened because of local demonstrations in support of the civil rights movement and later against the Vietnam War, providing opportunities for our speaking with the children about issues relating to the wider community. Inevitably, such opportunities arose at the children's, rather than the parents', convenience, often amidst the din of the family supper table, initially with two, then with six small children participating, listening in.

During that period of the civil rights movement, the deaths of John and Robert Kennedy, and the war in Vietnam, events were such that our children began asking questions about public issues rather early. Almost in spite of ourselves, my wife and I were drawn into discussions about poverty and discrimination, violence and war. The murder of John Kennedy made a deep impression on our younger son, for example, who told us later that as a result of that tragedy, he feared for our safety when we left the house, particularly when I participated in vigils or activities associated with the antiwar movement.

Although I am glad, in retrospect, that I had the good sense to try to stop that cruel and wasteful war, I realize that I should have been much more explicit in indicating my reasons for doing so. Young children, as well as some adults, do not necessarily understand why such activities are an integral part of the life and history of this country. How the society works, including how injustices have been eradicated in the past, is seldom explained to them. The impetus for my studying to be a draft counselor, for young men trying to make informed decisions about the Vietnam War and their participation in it, grew out of a concern about my own students, children of close friends, as well as my own sons. But it was a long time before I realized that a simple word or two to them about my work in draft counseling would have helped them make the connection between our values as parents and as citizens.

Children are, also, sometimes very sophisticated in making meaning of and in practicing the values they learn from parents. Years after the Vietnam War ended, I learned accidentally about my son's discussion with a neighbor we hardly knew, who asked him how he felt about the war. Partially as a result of my son's thoughtful response to that question, he and the lawyer, a customer on his paper route, became friends. Although I never remember discussing the issues with my son directly, he had apparently thought about them and formed some opinions of his own.

Although questions about values often emerge under less dramatic circumstances now than they did in the 1960s, the ones that prompted discussions among our children then are being asked today with even greater urgency. And the principle of taking advantage of issues as they come up, even at the most inopportune time, is still a good one. Moral lectures serve a purpose, in the home as well as in the classroom, but they seldom address the real ache at the moment it is fully felt.

Parents are wise to let events at school or on the playground—or when the children are older, headlines in the daily newspaper or on the evening news—determine the subjects for discussion at the dinner table: "So why do you think Ms. Sullivan next door made that remark about a black family moving in down the street?" As the children get a bit older, parents find themselves raising more complicated questions, some of them challenging parents' own beliefs and practices: "Is it really true," I found myself asking one of my daughters, "that regular churchgoers are hypocritical?" or "So why do you think I should get another job that pays more money, simply in order for us to buy fancier carpet for the living room?"

SUGGESTIONS FOR THE LONG HAUL

Teaching social values—or personal values, for that matter—means attending closely to children's responses every step of the way. It means respecting their strengths and accepting their weaknesses, building on the first and making generous allowances for the second; it means giving choices, suggesting alternatives, and learning as we go. In doing so, parents may find the following suggestions useful in laying the groundwork for the moral education of their children, and in helping them make sense of things as they grow.

1. *Begin teaching values early.* Children are never too young to reason with, and they often understand explanations long before adults think they do. As Carol Bly, author and mother of four, says, "They simply like to contemplate life and death." Robert Cormier, well-known author of children's books, agrees, saying, "They want to think, and they're handed so much pap." So it's as important to ask children questions as it is to give them answers: "Had you ever thought about death before Jimmy told you about his grandfather's funeral?" "What did you say to your classmate when she made that rude remark about black people?"

2. *Listen especially carefully to any statement of feelings.* If children say that they are frightened by lightning and thunder, by a particular person or event, believe them. Don't tell them *not* to feel a certain way. Instead, try to find out what caused their reactions and why, asking: "How did the sound of the thunder make you feel? Do you worry about the storm returning?" "Why do you cry when you see your father and me going out for the evening?" Be careful not to humiliate children, even when disciplining them. Whenever possible, be specific and generous with praise; also, an embrace or other gesture of affection, naturally given, speaks volumes.

3. *Take children's activities seriously.* Don't treat a child's first efforts as merely "nice." Recognize these efforts for what they are—the first, sometimes halting steps in his or her effort to become a maker, an artist, a doer. "We do not need to be told whether to be strict or permissive with our children," Alice Miller argues in a famous book about "poisonous pedagogy." She continues: "What we do need is to have respect for their needs, their feelings, and their individuality, as well as for our own." When they show you their drawings, ask questions about content: "What's the next step in the design or construction of your sand castle? Who lives there and what kind of work do they do?"

4. *Try to understand the significance of his or her actions within the context of the child's, rather than an adult's, world.* Yes, we

are often too exhausted or distracted to focus our attention on our children's concerns, and simply must resort to that well-worn command of tired parents: "Do it because I say so and that's an end of it." Children have their own culture. In their world, as well as in ours, balancing relationships and maintaining self-esteem influence the way they live their values at any given moment. Sometimes they may need help in maintaining their integrity, even at a very young age. Tom Paxton, who writes songs for children, describes a child's painful times in this way: "Being a kid is a very full experience. ... Certainly you have your moments of wonder, but it's a rough passage."

5. *Encourage children's abilities to solve problems on their own.* Resist telling them that they are too young or too inexperienced to "handle" a particular situation. Stand back, pray arduously, and hope for the best. Children need to grow up believing that they can think and can make their way through difficult situations. Remember, you did it, more often than not; and they will, too. Ruth Sanford, a long-time associate of the psychologist Carl Rogers, recommends "learning to love with an open hand." As she has grown older, Sanford says, she has realized that whenever "I impose my wish or want or try to exert power over another, I rob him or her of the full realization of growth and maturation." We sometimes limit and thwart by an act of possession, no matter how kind our intentions.

6. *Give precedence, usually, to the parents' relationship with one another.* When in doubt, allow for some benign neglect of the children, in order to sustain the family's welfare. All evidence indicates that children's values depend heavily upon how their father and mother treat one another. From that interaction, they learn what it means to be adult, what it means to be affectionate and responsible, what it means to be male and female. A young father of three, for example, remembers *his* father saying that in spite of difficulties and arguments, he always knew that his mom and dad loved one another. "That memory became important to me, too." Learning values means learning respect for other people's needs and rights and dignity, including those of one's parents.

7. *Never give up on your kids.* This valuable advice, offered on several occasions by a father of four, sustained me through many

worrisome moments: the afternoon a police officer appeared at our front door, one of our children in tow; the night a high-school counselor arrived at the same front door with another child, wobbly and glassy-eyed, obviously inebriated; the morning a long-distance call brought the news that one of the children had "totaled" our recently purchased used car. Remember, at such times: Tomorrow a new day dawns, with another chance for all of us to live responsibly.

Most of these "suggestions for the long haul," I realize, apply to parenting in general, not just to teaching social values. For that task, one must attend to other considerations that are complementary to, rather than in conflict with, personal values. Before making specific suggestions about how to do that, I want to look closely at the context within which parents teach values today, and at some new factors that make our task if not more difficult, at least rather different from the task of parents who went before.

2

THE CONTEXT

Set out in the world with no family, without story of and for the self, we will simply be captured by the reigning ideologies of the day.

— Stanley Hauerwas
"Peacemaking Is Conflict-making"

Whether parents are aware of it or not, the context for rearing children has been altered over the past twenty years: we and our children live in an America quite different from the one that went before. And our understanding of ourselves and our children depends, in part, upon our knowing and appreciating these differences.

Among the many factors affecting values in the home, the influence of television is surely one of the most immediate. No household invader occupies more time and space, proportionately, and none is more relentless than "the set" in its claim on the minds and imaginations—not to mention the physical posture—of our children.

For that reason, I decided to focus on television first, as a way of describing, perhaps actually *and* symbolically, the altered context for our teaching values in the home.

BEGINNING WITH TELEVISION

How little or how much television parents watch or allow their children to watch is sometimes one of the first episodes in a parent's efforts to guide a child in making choices. Holding out against viewing as long as possible, or allocating particular times when watching is permitted, may dampen a child's dependence upon the medium. Keeping the set out of the living room—in a crowded corner, in the basement, or on the second floor, whenever possible—tells children that you don't regard it as essential. It also prevents them (and us) from subjecting visitors to the rude practice of pretending to talk with them while eyes focus on the set.

When children become watchers, parents are wise to monitor the programs because of the shallow values projected by advertisements and silly sitcoms. Sometimes, too, they prompt conversations about what is or is not important. Such conversations won't even take place, however, unless someone simply turns off the set. "Since there is no specific memory of much of anything in the United States (or in any television culture)," as Gore Vidal wrote, parents are wise to give serious thought to "the television revolution" early on.

For one thing, television makes the human voice subordinate to other means of communicating ideas. Plot and dialogue are merely backdrops for the video image that imposes itself on the brain. Even in news reporting, the announcer's mindless prattle fills the air space that might be given to information and commentary on the day's events.

Second, television is a potentially addictive phenomenon, particularly through its advertising. The average American child watches six and one-half hours of television a day, and during that time children are deprived of important activities that contribute to cognitive development. As television advertising has become "more insidious, more persuasive, more a part of our everyday life, so it has become largely invisible," as Eric Clark has said. "Its images are taken for granted." Turning off the television may be the most important decision a parent makes in protecting a child's verbal and visual—and perhaps moral—imagination.

Simply turning it off may also keep parents from giving television more attention than it deserves. In itself, the medium is not all bad. The major claims against it may be not the crimes it commits against the tender psyches of children, through its hours of gossip, murders, and car crashes, but what it makes unlikely: silence, reading, word games, improvisations, long talks with friends, dressing up in parents' clothes—and all the other highly imitative and imaginative activities in which children ape and satirize and particularize for themselves the world they will eventually move into. If the world is a stage, childhood is occasionally a rehearsal time for trying out roles of being a man or woman. And don't we hope our children will choose *not* to be adult couch potatoes? The Industrial Workers of the World once put out posters proclaiming that child labor "steals the playtime of children." Today the same might be said of television.

It may also make children stupid. According to Jerome Singer, a child psychologist at Yale University, those who watch a great deal of television understand less of what they see than those who watch very little. They are also less able to follow a story line, to understand commercials, or to distinguish between fantasy and reality. Like their elders, children who watch television seem less willing to spend energy in creating their own images of the world; they rely on actors and news announcers to do that for them.

Television may not be the principal cause for rapid change in the social environment of children, but it certainly projects those changes in a dramatic way, and children's dependence upon it has a powerful effect on their sense of the world outside the home. George Orwell pointed out a half-century ago that popular culture may influence our values more fundamentally than so-called high culture.

Television offers considerable riches—and a handy distraction when a parent needs time off. Also, in a culture that relies less and less on reading as a means of knowledge, television sometimes provides an introduction to cultural artifacts—through dramatization of Greek or Hindu or Chinese myths, for example, or slightly altered modern versions of the same heroic and moral exploits; but it must be monitored and rationed if parents are to retain some control over the moral education of their children.

So even if the research on television's effect on children is not conclusive, the medium has undoubtedly become a force in forming our children's consciousness. And as Jerome and

Dorothy Singer ask, on the basis of their research, "Wouldn't it make more sense ... if parents knew what their children were watching and under what circumstances?" In regard to caring for a child's moral and imaginative development, they concluded (not surprisingly) that "the growing child is nurtured best through the relationship with a warm, communicating parent and not through passive exposure to an electronic screen."

What one decides about television has broad social implications, since it is formative in the life of many American children. How infuriating, I used to think, as a parent—and now think, as a grandparent—that decisions about this postmodernist invader must be regarded as so basic a part of "the task" of parenting. But there television and videos are, setting the context, even as we try to focus on more pressing responsibilities.

THE NATIONAL SCENE

As parents, we find ourselves teaching values at a time of rapid social change—the result of economic and political upheaval, of imperial ambition and its consequences. Since the 1970s, particularly, Americans have supported "a negative, uncompassionate role for government," as John Kenneth Galbraith has said, resulting in the rich greatly increasing their share of income and the poor being denied basic needs of shelter, education, and medical care.

Radically increased military expenditures, eating away at the resources of this country, undermine social programs in health and education. Many college graduates, especially physicists and engineers, face job markets in which up to 70 percent of the openings are with war industries. Young couples, their incomes down by 25 percent since 1973, can no longer afford down payments or closing costs for a home—a trend, according to Harvard's Joint Center for Housing Studies, that may produce "a permanent underclass of disadvantaged renters." Many Americans, including two million children, are homeless.

In trying to understand the social structures within which our teaching children to be good takes place, I take seriously the testimony of so-called high culture as well as popular culture—books, films, television documentaries, governmental and nongovernmental reports, and advertisements. All show a society characterized by confusion and injustice and people in pain, as the gap widens between rich and poor. The daily newspaper and television specials tell stories of young parents and children charting the course of their lives through the hazardous waste and uncertain economic terrain of American culture. "Why is this so?" many have asked. Because the actual cost of "making it," as Michael Lerner has said, depended upon "a highly individualistic society in which community ties had been replaced by the struggle of each against all."

In the early 1990s, the contrasts among the upper, middle, and lower classes are more dramatic than ever, with the upper 1 percent of the population owning more than the lower 90 percent of the population combined. Regrettably, also, in foreign and domestic policy, violence is regarded as a first (rather than a last) resort in resolving conflict.

Within recent memory, for example, the Reagan administration ordered the bombing of Libya, killing many innocent people; the navy shot down an unarmed passenger plane over the Persian Gulf; George Bush and the Congress sent $400 million to a military government in El Salvador that was complicit in murdering seventy thousand people over the previous ten years; and the Bush administration directed the invasion of Panama, killing hundreds of civilians. Such facts, often relegated to the periphery in discussions of parenting, are relevant, it seems to me, if we are to understand why particular tasks of parents today appear more demanding—if not more difficult—than similar tasks of their ancestors. As a grandparent, I am more aware of that connection now than I was when our children were young.

Parents in any period of history endure certain adversities— and enjoy certain rewards—associated with having young children. Watching young couples with six-month-old babies, I remember and momemtarily relive those demanding first months: my wife's readjusting after the pregnancy's assault on her body chemistry; my own confusion and uncertainty about feelings of displacement and awesome responsibilities—and both of us physically exhausted from being up all hours of the night.

For a while, mothers and fathers quite naturally treat social and political issues as distant, peripheral. But increasingly, particularly in recent decades, the larger world impinges upon elemental tasks. Young couples speak of their reluctance to marry, for example, until they have accumulated substantial savings and household furnishings, or to have children unless the same conditions are met.

Making the necessary links between our vocation as parents and our lives as citizens may keep us not only from blaming ourselves for certain "failures," but also from shirking certain tasks essential to our own welfare. In the midst of struggling with problems associated with fewer job opportunities for themselves, higher prices for basic consumer goods, and a weakened public school system for their children, parents occasionally think they *personally* are at fault, not the economic and political system sometimes responsible for these conditions.

One historian, in giving a half-century perspective on the shift in national priorities, pointed to these significant facts: (1) in 1939, America's army numbered 185,000 men, with no troops in any foreign country and an annual budget of less that $500 million; (2) in 1989, it numbered 1.5 million men and women, with troops in over one hundred foreign countries and an annual budget of over $300 billion.

At the same time, a pervasive pain, perhaps linked to grief, has weakened the general public's will to alter the priorities of government and to redirect the agencies and institutions associated with it. Following Reagan's and Bush's cuts in funding for education and social welfare, only the children of the rich enjoy opportunities once taken for granted by the middle class. No wonder young parents—and grandparents—feel as if their progeny's opportunities for full participation in the wider culture are increasingly limited.

For related reasons, basic needs of children at various stages of development are simply not being met; and many are deprived of the joys associated with childhood and a generally supportive environment so crucial to growing up. Rich or poor or in-between, they today contend with some of the greatest stresses ever, according to pediatricians, psychologists, and teachers.

In a survey of American teenagers in 1986, for example, over half of the students interviewed named nuclear war as their number one fear, a concern shared by public school children regardless of age, sex, race, religion, class, and politics. Referring to what he called an "alarming degree of futurelessness" among young Americans, Dr. Eric Chivian, Harvard Medical School, director of the study, said that the students felt that many of the problems we face aren't solvable. "Despair breeds inaction and that's the most serious problem of all," he added. Not surprisingly, teenagers in the Soviet Union shared the same fears as their American contemporaries.

Although it is difficult to gauge accurately, young Americans of college age endure a similar anger and despair, if I can judge by my own experience in the classroom. Depression is something one senses in conversations with students, rather than fully understands, although teachers and counselors emphasize it enough to make me think it is common. In recent years, anxiety about "life after college" and strictures of the job market have increased to an inordinate degree.

For example, speaking with a former student — an intelligent, talented athlete about to enter law school — about the decisions he and other seniors faced during their last semester in college, I got this representative response: "Perhaps my roommate summed it up best when he said, 'I can work for Dow Chemical, pollute the streams, and kill the fish for $50,000 a year, or I can save the streams and fish, work for the Environmental Protection Agency, and live as a pauper.' Fortunately, thanks to a four-year commitment to Army R.O.T.C., he has four years to decide his course. In the meantime, he's into binary chemical weapons, but that's another topic for another time."

Making allowances for the special circumstances of a graduating senior, one can still recognize the choice he mentions as representative of the military/industrial/university dilemma faced by many young people. Worried about a heavy indebtedness because of his college loans and an uncertain job market in education or the social services, he looks out on what appears to be a narrow range of choices. The fact that there are alternatives to the two he mentions may seem obvious to experienced adults. But unless a young person has heard about or directly experienced these alternatives, he or she may not be willing to take a risk. Unless, as parents, we help to create a kind of "nuclear free zone," in the midst of increasing social and economic pressure, our children may view the future with similar blinders.

Growing up in the Reagan era, many young people reason that the "fashionable acquisitiveness of the 1980s" or "the sneaky pursuit of the dollar" is the only way to go, particularly if they have had no firsthand knowledge and no encouragement from parents or other adults about other options. One may suggest to young people (as I did to the young man mentioned above) that they might still earn a decent salary working in any number of social services that do not pollute the environment or feed the war industry. But it will take a chorus of authoritative voices—and more public support for "peace" professions and industries—to get them to explore those possibilities, particularly if their family, their peers, and the country's leadership insist that the race belongs only to the swift, the cunning, and the unethical.

The fact that Oliver North managed to wangle the entire $25,000 annual budget from the student government of a leading Catholic university for one speech says something significant about the effects of double-dealing in Washington and public morals. At the same time, Wasserman, the political cartoonist for the *Boston Globe*, caricatured Oliver North's lecturing youngsters in a back alley and saying, appropriately, "Listen up, kids—first, don't get caught . . . if caught, don't admit guilt . . . and if found guilty, say it was someone else's idea."

Speaking more directly about his generation, the graduating senior (mentioned above) added, "Apparently the apathetic atmosphere of today's youth is rooted in avarice, but it is not so much *greed* in the 'evil' sense as it is the fear of living in a dumpster that makes us this way. I think people feel that unless they continue to hustle and 'look out for number one' they could end up with nothing." The folksinger Greg Brown, in "Just a Bum," describes this fear of losing everything in the following two lines: "Time ain't money / when all you got is time." Is this not a new phenomenon among young Americans? As the economy deteriorates and we tolerate priorities favoring militarism over education, housing, and health care, will the fears of young men and women of the present generation only increase in the years ahead? Is this not another reason for giving serious thought to alternative ways of thinking and behaving for ourselves and for our children? Of considerable importance, also, is this question: How might we suggest those alternatives to young people in as nonthreatening a manner as possible?

BASIC QUESTIONS

In teaching values to their children, parents are likely to face several basic questions, including: (1) How can we teach our children about justice and nonviolence in a culture dominated increasingly by the politics of greed and violence? (2) How might our children learn generosity and community when vanity and competition are the order of the day? and (3) Is there a more authentic tradition than the one served up by the dominant culture that might sustain us in this effort? In the following chapters, I try to respond to these questions as directly and simply as possible. Before doing so, I want to describe representative ways in which these questions arise for today's parents and to mention a few general approaches for addressing them.

The experience of a father of four, a naval airforce veteran, a physician, and an avid Green Bay Packers' fan, suggests, perhaps, the changes in context between being a parent today and in a previous generation. A thoughtful, conscientious person (but up to that point only indirectly involved in social issues), he agreed, in 1987, to accompany a group of doctors bringing medical supplies to Nicaragua. It was his first close look at the consequences of U.S. foreign policy in a Third World country. Although the medical personnel in Nicaragua were as well-trained as he, medical supplies—in part because of the U.S. economic boycott against Nicaragua—were almost nonexistent. The two-week experience shook him in a way that he never expected, and, returning home, he visited the offices of every person in his state's congressional delegation to lobby for a change in U.S. policy toward Central America.

Further reading and discussion in the weeks that followed merely confirmed this middle-age father's sense of having been betrayed by his own government. He also felt ignorant, even a sense of self-hatred, for knowing so little about the conditions

endured by others as a result of the carelessness and cruelty of
U.S. policy. He also wondered what *his* father would have done
in such circumstances, only to remember that his father almost
inevitably went along with whatever the U.S. government did.
As far as he knew, his father had never questioned the Cold
War rhetoric that had characterized U.S. policy for over forty
years. What models were there for maintaining a love of country,
yet opposing its behavior toward much of the rest of the world?
How could he convey to his sons and daughters a sense of American tradition when he felt so in conflict with much of what it
represented?

Caught between a love of his native land and a profound
distrust of its stance toward Central America, this parent confronted directly the differences between his father's time and
his own. As with many of us growing up in the 1950s or even
the 1960s, he probably could not even name the countries of
Central America, much less describe social conditions in the
region, where an alliance among wealthy landowners, the military, American businesses, and armed forces have kept 80 percent of the people in poverty.

This father had reached his midfifties before he came to
appreciate the dichotomy between the White House's description of his country's stance toward Central America and the
actual condition. Becoming aware of the gap between official
policy and the truth led him at one point to the brink of despair.
Recovering his composure, he set for himself a course of action
and carried through on it; he changed his life, not without effort
and considerable pain. In the process, he sometimes felt alienated from his friends because of his own inability to communicate his true feelings about his time in Central America and also
because of his friends' attempts to keep him and his "bad news"
at a distance.

I mention these liabilities of living in conflict with the dominant culture as a kind of warning. For in educating children to
be "citizens of the world," parents place them, at times, in difficult situations. For that reason, we need to prepare children
as best we can for the lack of understanding and appreciation
of their point of view that may arise from others on occasion.
As always, one proceeds with caution, so that any values we

teach become theirs not by their echoing us, but by their choosing them for themselves.

MAKING SENSE

Helping children make sense of their lives is one of the central tasks of moral education, in social as well as personal values. And the best way of helping children make sense is talking and listening to them--that is, taking them seriously—from the moment they are born. As a baby's eyes begin to focus, its head moves toward sound: responding to speech, its soul seems to come alive, moment-by-moment, before our very eyes. And someone four years old (or any age?) is given dignity the moment someone asks him or her a question and takes time to attend to the answer. "Where is that spaceship flying to that you've just drawn on the paper? Why did you color it red? What is the pilot saying to the people when she looks out the window?" And so on.

Young children usually respond to questions (and answers) if they are used to being talked to or read to, that is, if their own initiatives have evoked other responses. From the very beginning, children make meaning as they go. Asked why they act as they do, they "invent," as problem solvers on the spot. Being responded to gives them an opportunity to think over, around, and through their reasons for taking action. In speaking to them, parents tell children, most important of all, that what they think matters. And even a distracted response is better than none.

In teaching values, as in teaching language, we must employ every method in the book—repetition, commentary, and personal example—if we want our children to be honest, truthful, and courteous in their personal dealings with others. A friend of mine, a mother of three, stressed this point in recounting a story of her children's amazement when she treated her rough-hewn paper boy courteously, though many people regarded him as a roughneck, perhaps even a hoodlum. Years later, her grown children cited this incident as proof that their mother really believed her dictum, often repeated to them, about the value of every person.

THE BELOVED COMMUNITY

Teaching responsibility for people further removed from our field of vision, in the global village, is more difficult, as I suggest in chapter 9. Even in a pluralistic society which tries to respect cultural, ethnic, and religious differences, however, one must make a conscious effort to introduce children to various ways of being in the world.

Increasingly, groups of people in American society isolate themselves from one another, as the divisions between rich and poor become more pronounced. Although we have laws against discrimination and segregation, as well as state and local agencies to carry out these laws, many of us still grow up, attend colleges and universities, and settle into work and leisure routines without ever forming friendships with people whose color, national origin, neighborhood, or region differ significantly from our own.

So one must make a conscious effort to see that "the others," whether minorities in this country or the poor in other parts of the world, do not become invisible. Helping children—and ourselves—become citizens of the world means "seeing" in our mind's eye whoever is not immediately visible. Who will lose their homes in any downtown area marked for gentrification? What Central American workers were exploited or thrown off their land to provide hamburger or coffee for U.S. homes and fast-food restaurants? How many maintenance workers were exposed to cancer because of the careless administrators at a nearby nuclear power plant?

Remaining conscious of these "others" takes some discipline, first of all, on the part of parents. Trying to make them part of the home scene and a child's world is more difficult. In doing that, we need to redefine our task in certain ways and eventually to learn a new language and new approaches to being good parents.

Children, like adults, are often unaware of their power to affect the world around them. In treating children seriously, we help them to become conscious of how their behavior affects themselves, as well as others, and how they can gain some control over their own environment.

In the home as in the school or the community, parents can clarify issues and make unwritten rules explicit, including rules that need to be changed. Even at a very young age, children develop a sense of whether what they say or do matters in how the family governs itself. After waiting too long to initiate the practice, I was struck by the immediate effect of our family meetings at suppertime, which furthered everyone's understanding of what the family was about. Almost inevitably, those discussions reduced the conflicts and petty squabbles among siblings as well as their resistance to doing household chores. As I indicate in chapter 8, such a simple practice provided affirmation for the younger children, who had seldom gotten equal time, apparently, in previous family gatherings. Long afterward, I realized that my wife and I were merely applying what are regarded as basic social-worker skills relating to empathy and acceptance; I wish I had known about such skills years earlier.

With some practice at home, children understand, once they go to school, that "put-downs" are merely another means by which others, in the classroom or on the playground, keep power over them and that, sometimes, the situation need not remain so discouraging and disheartening. Several of our children, for example, dreaded moving from their small, neighborhood grammar school to the large, intimidating junior high school, until they discovered that, with the help of others, they might stand up to rowdies whom their classmates feared as much as they did. Working together, children can alter conditions by undercutting those currents that encourage a bully or a tyrant-in-the-making.

Understanding the context in which we form and live out our values is the first step in developing a coherent rationale in teaching our children; the next step is altering that context, so that what we regard as important can be communicated to and understood by those we are trying to teach. Changing our condition makes it necessary for us to behave as citizens—not by passive acceptance of but by active involvement in structuring family life and, perhaps, restructuring our communities.

In contemporary American culture, basic injustices render

the context for living potentially or actually violent. Since violence is a destructive reaction to conflict, skills in resolving conflict are essential to our functioning as citizens, particularly if we wish to build a society—including a home life—so well described by Martin Luther King, in 1957, as "the beloved community."

But also, since conflict is an essential aspect of life—in the family, the school, and the community—learning to understand its proper place in the scheme of things and the various means of reconciling it are central to practicing social values, as the following chapter suggests.

PART II

AUTHENTIC WAYS
OF BEING

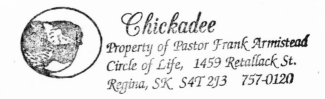

3

MAKING PEACE

Since every family faces internal and external conflicts and tensions, how they are resolved will serve as powerful lessons in peacemaking.

—Sidney Callahan
"Foreword," *Homemade Social Justice*

Rapid nuclear disarmament ... is the ultimate parenting issue.

—Helen Caldicott
Missile Envy

In the family, as in the United Nations, making peace means principally resolving conflict. For "peace is not merely the absence of war," in the words of the papal encyclical *Gaudium et Spes*, "it is rightly and appropriately called 'an enterprise of justice.'"

Properly understood, neither peacemaking nor nonviolence tolerates "passivity" as a response to injustice. Rather, each actively resists injustice, as Stanley Hauerwas has said, "by confronting the wrongdoer with the offer of reconciliation." For this reason, among others, peacemaking is central to the moral education of children, and to a mother and father's efforts to contain and to heal the constant disruptions associated with parenting.

Even the birth of a child, for example, upsets the equilibrium

of the family, as a young couple struggles with the new challenges associated with late-night feedings, diapering, and welcoming a new member of the group. Parceling out household
and child-rearing responsibilities, when both husband and wife
work outside the home, requires as much time and effort, it
seems, as negotiating international disputes. In settling sibling
rivalries and neighborhood squabbles, as the children grow
older, a parent employs skills in mediation and conflict resolution that any labor leader or management consultant might envy.

Deciding who gets to sit by the window during a drive in the
country or, later, who can use the family car for a weekend date
puts a parent in the place of judge, jury, and probation officer
within minutes of "trying" the case. Maintaining peace in the
family, therefore, requires some planning, a division of labor,
and a willingness to cooperate and to compromise on essential
tasks.

Parents' efforts to "keep the peace" among various members,
from early childhood through adulthood, as with so many other
aspects of teaching values, dramatize the interdependency of
people at every level. Paying close attention to the dynamics of
that enterprise prepares adults as well as children to function
as citizens in the wider community. Teaching a child how to
confront the schoolyard bully or how to respond to an oppressive
teacher or employer is an important exercise in peacemaking;
so is his or her participation in a vigil or march against a local
arms manufacturer or polluter of the local water supply.

Much of the debate over how best to function as a peacemaker, however, centers on the very concept of peace, since
peace has positive and negative connotations. Although peace
depends upon good management, orderly resolution of conflict,
harmony, gentleness, and love, it also mistakenly implies the
absence of tension, conflict, excitement, and vigor. Is that why
artists have such a difficult time providing visual representations
of peace? In art history, one thinks immediately of all the powerful renderings of war, including the heroic portraits of David
and the bitter denunciations of war by Goya and Picasso.
Whereas, aside from Edward Hicks's *The Peaceable Kingdom*
and the pastoral scenes of Constable, portraits of peace are
characteristically static, not to say boring.

Peace in any setting requires a balance of forces. For that reason, parents maintaining peace in the home or in the wider community know that they must be active, vigilant, and resourceful at critical moments. Peacemaking, in fact, resembles a complicated juggling act involving many players and considerable art; it is also, in the words of the economist Kenneth Boulding, "quite consistent with conflict and excitement, debate and dialogue, drama and confrontation." In any setting, however, these processes must not get out of hand, as Boulding says, lest becoming pathological, they cause more trouble than they are worth.

Peace can be *imposed*, in other words, by the threat of force or even terror, but that is hardly a stable peace, since its basis is repression. A tyrannical father or mother can silence a household by the threat of violence ("Answer me back once more and I'll make you sorry you ever said a word"); or a nation can impose a Pax Romana by economic and military dominance. Functioning in this way, a parent may ignore the psychological consequences to the children (or a government may ignore the human rights of citizens). In such instances, neither "ruler" provides a healthy environment for his or her "subjects." Peace is tenuous at best, and the consequences, including physical and psychological harm, become evident only later on.

I emphasize the similarities between maintaining peace at home and in the world for two reasons. First, because they are sometimes ignored; and second, because thinking through an approach to peace in the family is useful in "imaging" a new social order. Each involves learning a "new" language, a process that has been described by various activists and writers. In a poem called "Making Peace," Denise Levertov says that such a process

> can't be known except
>   in the words of its making, . . .
>   A feeling towards it,
> dimly sensing a rhythm, is all we have
> until we begin to utter its metaphors,
> learning them as we speak.

THE LANGUAGE OF WAR, THE LANGUAGE OF PEACE

Even if the values we espouse regarding peace resemble those of an earlier time, we may need to learn new ways of understanding and communicating them if they are to affect the lives of our children. The times have changed; the social and political issues are different and perhaps more complicated; and the pressures on our children have increased, as I tried to suggest in chapter 2. Peacemaking may remain "merely personal" — peripheral to our daily lives, with no implications for the social order — unless we make some important connections.

How can we convince our sons and daughters of the importance of resolving conflict by nonviolent means, for example, when corporations and professions consistently reward manipulation and violence? How effectively can we argue against our children playing with guns when President Bush bows to a well-financed gun lobby that encourages selling arms to almost anyone who wishes to buy them? What child will listen to a lecture on the value of honesty and forthrightness when officials in high places condone or support "secret wars" in defiance of our elected representatives?

An increase in violence in the family is directly related to altered patterns in family life in recent history, I would argue, as well as to the warmaking and aggression that have characterized American foreign policy since World War II. Is it possible to alleviate violence inside the United States without giving up our role as one of the two major suppliers of armaments to other countries of the world? Can any American raise his or her voice against increased violence in homes and communities without speaking clearly, as Martin Luther King said in 1967, "to the greatest purveyor of violence in the world today — my own government"?

In a culture that has become almost immune to the difference between conflict and violence, we often forget that nonviolence is the proper means, and reconciliation the proper end, of all controversy. In this, as in so many other matters, our very language betrays us when we use images of war and violence in referring to relatively minor differences in point of view.

In his description of the first television debate between George Bush and Michael Dukakis, during the presidential campaign of 1988, for example, a journalist said that although Governor Dukakis had probably "won" the debate, the governor had "failed to deliver the knock-out punch." Was the journalist suggesting that candidates for the presidency can best exhibit their qualifications for the nation's highest office by pulverizing their opponents?

In previous administrations as well as the present one, presidents have talked about their programs addressing poverty and drugs as "wars." When George Bush called for an "assault on every front" against drugs, a Democratic senator countered that we need "another D-Day, not another Vietnam," and his Republican colleague added that "it's a war on drugs, not a war on the American taxpayer." The problem with such talk, as Ellen Goodman points out, is that "metaphor makes the mind-set," implying that there is "only one set of responses to a myriad number of situations: violence. ... It emphasizes enemies and not allies, combatants and not civilians, aggression and not protection, destruction over building."

In recent films (and television programs), parents and children are subjected each day to a staggering increase in metaphors and images of violence. By the age of eight, many young people have seen 80,000 homicides and numerous brutal beatings in the media. The hero or heroine of such dramatizations often succeeds by employing the violent means of the adversary, much as the allied powers defeated Hitler by resorting to massive bombings and murder of civilian populations in World War II. By injesting Hitler's rationale—becoming, in the process, the most powerful nation in the world, four times over—America's policymakers and even its citizenry seemed, at times, to adopt his total war ethic.

Since 1980, in the inevitable decline of U.S. dominance (though not necessarily its influence) over much of the world, Americans have tended to define our relationship with other nations as a competition, usually understood in military terms. Even in the Olympics, the victory of an American athlete or team is seen as proof of American superiority in the world.

At such times, one becomes aware of the need for a new language and terminology and perhaps for new myths regarding peace, that is, a body of stories about people who define themselves as partners, rather than as competitors, in an international community. A new language and new stories, many of them drawn from alternative traditions already available to us, might convey to children a different set of values from those paraded before them in public life and on television.

Every cultural tradition is replete with stories and sayings about living in peace—the good Samaritan, from the New Testament, and the sayings of various Hindu, Chinese, African, and Native American sages. The early Christians emphasized, for example, the differences between the example of Jesus and that of earlier prophets. "The Lord, in disarming Peter, ungirded every soldier," said Tertullian, a theologian of the third century. "We, who used to kill one another, do not make war on our enemies," said Justin, shortly afterward. Francis of Assisi, in the thirteenth century, forbad his followers to bear arms. A tradition of peacemakers in the United States, from the early Quakers to the present, includes sayings such as this one, by A. J. Muste: "There is no way to peace; peace is the way." In his sermon "Loving Your Enemies," given in Montgomery, Alabama, at Christmas 1957, Martin Luther King advanced a similar argument during the nonviolent struggle for civil rights.

FAMILY CONFLICT

People's longing and efforts for peace are natural to all cultures; so is the presence of conflict. Conflict is so basic to family life—and indeed to human life—that it inevitably involves children at a very young age. Negotiating between competing interests in the home (Who hit whom? For what reason? Under what circumstances?) is as basic to peacemaking as settling border disputes between China and the Soviet Union, Canada and the United States. And the means of resolving such conflicts are not so different. Both activities tax the energies of all parties involved, calling for patience, restraint, and quick decisions that may either dissipate or heighten the violence implicit in the incident.

In the family, conflicts often arise under the most surprising circumstances and, almost inevitably, at the wrong time. Once, for example, one of our younger children upset a next-door neighbor by running his truck through her flowerbed, his older brother provoked the ire of a middle-age man across the street by rightfully challenging his false accusation about tracking mud across his living room carpet. When our son spoke to him in a firm but polite manner, the man struck the child in the face — not injuring him, but deeply humiliating him. Using brute force was, unfortunately, the man's customary manner of dealing with conflict in his house.

My son, enraged and in tears, resolved to punish the man by retaliating in the same way. In subsequent discussions with my son, it was clear that my speaking with the man about the incident was not enough. Unsure about the next step, I saw the potentiality for serious psychological harm to him if I treated the incident lightly.

Ultimately, I settled on asking a lawyer friend to discuss with my son the possible legal alternatives available; I hoped, of course, that he would not insist upon that, but wanted that to be his decision, not mine. The lawyer's intervention, including his attentive, concrete discussion of available alternatives, helped to alleviate the boy's feeling of powerlessness in dealing with a tyrannical neighbor. Such complicated mediations are the necessary means, sometimes, of making peace in the neighborhood and in the world. Would that all mediations between conflicting parties were half as successful as that one.

An important distinction to keep in mind in making peace is the one between conflict and violence. Conflict is natural, perhaps inevitable in almost any human setting; violence is not.

Violent feelings, also, are natural, as most folktales and children's stories, from ancient times to the present, suggest. And perhaps the best way of acknowledging that fact is to treat seriously a child's feelings of anger and rage from the time he or she is an infant. In contemporary culture, this takes some doing because violence, as such, is accepted as inevitable, ignored or treated casually, practically encouraged. Any doubt about the casualness with which the subject is treated can be erased in a few minutes of watching prime-time television, where the psyche is violated and bombarded numerous times every minute by noise, manipulation, harassment, and insult.

In almost every advertisement, great liberties are taken with the human spirit, and every device and trick are used to achieve what is often a very undesirable end—to get a person to buy what is not needed, in fact what is often harmful to one's health: processed foods; sugar-coated, nonnutritious food; hair spray propelled by gases that damage the ozone in the atmosphere; war toys that validate an atmosphere of violence that a parent hopes to discourage.

As a subject, violence is, thus, too central to life and literature not to try to understand its fascination for human beings. A parent wisely considers ways of channeling energy evoked by violent feelings into constructive action, as Bruno Bettelheim and other psychologists have recommended. Our paying close attention to violent feelings and attitudes in our children leads naturally to our considering the sources of violence in ourselves and others, and ways of preventing those feelings from ending in violent actions.

One preventive measure, in saying no to the culture's endorsement of violence among children, is resisting the hard-sell media tactics for selling war toys, and refusing to buy the ugly, expensive, and destructive junk available each Christmas at the local Toys R Us or department store. While it is true that children denied guns may ingeniously manufacture their own, by using sticks or metal rods or their own thumb and forefinger, they at least won't be riding through the living room in motorized tanks firing rubber bullets at their siblings and neighborhood friends.

PARENT AS PEACEMAKER

Psychologically, the principle of peacemaking can often be understood best through a family model, as I mentioned earlier, one frequently used in mediating between and among various members. A parent's awareness of the connecting links—father to mother, father to son, mother to son, father to daughter, mother to daughter, son to daughter, etc.—helps her or him to understand the dynamics of family relationships and to mediate rivalries that sometimes exist almost from the minute a young child enters the scene.

Maintaining peace in the family, like maintaining peace in the community, requires giving each person his or her due. Here, as elsewhere, Martin Luther King's counsel on making peace is pertinent: "Peace is not the absence of conflict, but the presence of justice."

An insistence upon everyone in the family being given a chance to speak and upon the right of everyone to be listened to, without interruption, is a necessary beginning. My wife and I were a long time learning this, and only got around to it as the children approached adolescence. Only then did we realize how, in the rush of events, the younger children were increasingly drowned out at a noisy dinner table. Almost inevitably, as discussions progressed, the older, more articulate ones interrupted or talked louder in order to seize the initiative. (Later on, family meetings, as I point out in chapter 8, helped to solve that dilemma.)

As children venture out into the neighborhood and attend school, the issues of peacemaking become even more complicated. With boys or girls, a parent almost inevitably deals with the threat of violence, sometimes perpetrated by a neighborhood tough or one's own child. Sometimes a child begins to lose confidence because of the threat posed by another; or word reaches you from neighborhood parents that your son has threatened to beat up their son.

In most cases, one must intervene, in the interests of all, or at the very least must keep close watch on how such conflicts resolve themselves. Whatever the situation, the matter of a child's respect for himself or herself and for the other person is central. And what Martin Luther King said regarding disputes between nations is equally true regarding those between a husband and wife, parents and children, or one household and another: "Life and history give eloquent testimony to the fact that conflicts are never resolved without trustful give and take on both sides."

A young black student's questions prompted one of the best discussions of this topic I ever heard. Asked, "Would you ever run away from a fight?" Dr. Bernard LaFayette, a veteran civil rights leader and apostle of nonviolence, answered, "Although I would not recommend running away from a fight, I can offer no guarantee that if you stand your ground you can avoid being hurt." Following that realistic assessment of the consequences, he then offered some specific advice in resisting violence, non-violently, by using moral force against the physical force of an opponent. Practically, he also emphasized maintaining eye contact with one's opponent as a way of conveying one's concern, even in argument, for the other person.

Dr. LaFayette shifted the focus of the discussion not by ignoring the likelihood of having to confront an opponent, but by insisting upon the importance of moral character and of the spiritual or psychological dimension of any attempt at dealing with conflict. (In extreme cases, helping a child settle a dispute with the neighborhood bully may make it necessary for a parent to teach a child to defend himself or herself physically.) Either way, the center of a parent's teaching nonviolence to children is teaching respect for the other person, as well as themselves, and discouraging all violent or oppressive means of settling disputes.

Building stable peace in any context calls for a kind of religious commitment by the mediator and sometimes by all the parties involved. One tries, in such circumstances, to follow what appear to be conflicting counsels, "to do justice" and "to forgive enemies." The first often requires us to make conflicts that are hidden public, and thus to risk provoking anger; the second requires us to pardon offenses ("seventy times seven") that are already public and to renounce violence. Marriages survive only through constant, mutual efforts at peacemaking. Families — and friendships and all other cooperative endeavors — depend upon a similar dedication to absolve differences in a manner that preserves the integrity of everyone.

The means of maintaining peace in families is obviously a very large subject, touched only briefly here. And through the work of many people in the social sciences, including whole schools of family systems theory and conflict resolution, we are learning a great deal more about the skills essential to the art. Much of their work dramatizes important links between positive peace in the home and in the wider community, and why preparation in one setting enables us to achieve similar goals in another.

CITIZEN AS PEACEMAKER

In the long effort to think our way through to new priorities for our country, discussions among parents, friends, and associates from differing points of view will inevitably evoke disagreements. One can attribute such conflicts regarding the subject of peace to at least three causes: (1) the fact that many of us feel terribly vulnerable in a nuclear age—not knowing when we will be blown up; (2) the fact that many of us wish to make a positive contribution to peacemaking, but have little opportunity to talk with someone about the complex issues involved; and (3) the fact that—even when we agree that "something must be done"—we are not sure how or where our participation can really make a difference.

In teaching a course for undergraduate students on the rhetoric of peace, for example, I became aware of the urgency with which questions about war or peace affect the daily lives of young men and women. Each of them had a great deal to say on the issues; each had a "philosophy" of war and peace, though it usually took some time for it to emerge, and only after they began to trust one another. They needed to know, for example, that they would not be laughed at or scorned if they spoke honestly and forcefully about their own "prescription for peace."

One person might be convinced that the only hope for peace was for the United States to impose it on the rest of the world, a kind of Pax Americana, backed up by the threat of first strike. Another person might be convinced that the only hope for peace was for the United States to disarm unilaterally, and thus provide an example to the rest of the world. Another person might feel the situation was hopeless and the only thing to do was simply to hope against hope that no one would "press the button." Yet, in most instances, all defended their positions vigorously and were sometimes quite threatened by anyone who conscientiously espoused (or worse, lived) values in conflict with their own.

Gradually, I came to see that my first responsibility, as the adult member of the discussion, was to make sure that each person had a chance to present his or her point of view without undue interference from others, particularly after I realized that people were not listening to one another. The participants blocked out one another not because they were excessively rude or intolerant, but because each was so convinced that he or she held the key to peace. As I gained more experience in refereeing these conflicts and in speaking with others about the nuclear arms race, I began to understand the complicated psychological process that makes discussions of the harsh realities of war and peace in our time so troublesome for everyone involved. And I began to feel that one contribution I could make was simply to sit and listen, first of all, to each person's perspective, before asking him or her to entertain an alternative point of view.

Such advice may seem terribly obvious or basic (and it is). But I think in dealing with adults, the issues related to peace call for a great deal of restraint. The same is true, though for different reasons, in approaching them with children, as I try to suggest in my cautionary note at the end of chapter 8.

Two crucial values in "making peace" are patience and persistence. When Daniel Berrigan, poet and war resister, described patience as "a revolutionary virtue," his context was the Vietnam War, and he was referring both to the Vietnamese people who were resisting foreign aggression and to antiwar activists in the United States. Berrigan's point applies equally to any on-going effort for peacemaking—in settling a dispute in the family, in arbitration with labor and management, and in mediation among people with conflicting views about peace and war.

Persistence is another crucial aspect of a good peacemaker. A violent culture never lacks hardliners counseling punishment of children and other offenders "for their own good." So parents must be imaginative and long-suffering in counseling peace when there is no peace. And citizens must be imaginative and long-suffering in keeping a vision of a world without war, and they must do so through the various means at their disposal: at times, by silent witness and cooperative programs; at others, by educational campaigns in schools, churches, and community centers; at times by direct confrontation of and nonviolent resistance against those in power.

•

The United States has been at war so long—moving directly from World War II to the Cold War, with interventions in Korea, Southeast Asia, repeatedly in the Caribbean and Central America, as well as through ideological confrontations with the Soviet Union—that we have only a limited familiarity with, and understanding of, the language of peace. And for a significant percentage of the American people, war is "big business," at times perhaps our major business.

A senior professor at West Point was quoted as saying, for example, in response to major changes in Central Europe and the break up of the communist block: "I sense a great deal of ambivalence over world events among the officer corps. As soldiers we have to be happy about rapprochement with the Soviet Union and the prospects of long-term peace. . . . But then the thought comes, 'My God. This could mean my job.' "

A half-century commitment to warmaking calls for a similar long-term, sustained, and in-depth commitment to peacemaking in the years ahead. We might begin, as I suggested earlier, by learning the language of peace, in a manner described in Denise Levertov's poem cited earlier, knowing that

> peace, like a poem,
> is not there ahead of itself,
> can't be imagined before it is made,
> can't be known except
> in the words of its making,
> grammar of justice,
> syntax of mutual aid.

The home is a proper place for parents to begin "studying" that language—patiently, persistently—in order to teach its grammar and syntax to our children. Committed to that language, we can then use it in resolving the conflicts at the center of our own lives and of the common life that we share with a larger community.

4

UNDERSTANDING
FATHERHOOD

Rhesus monkeys and human males can become good
fathers, if they put their minds to the task, . . . but it takes
a long time, full of trial and error.
> — Alice S. Rossi
> "The Biosocial Side of Parenthood"

The father who loves his son and makes it known, even in
the sorriest circumstances, lifts the child to a privileged
order from which he can never be expelled.
> — Gloria Emerson
> *Some American Men*

Teaching children the language of nonviolence, in a culture
that neither speaks nor understands it, absorbs much of our
energy and patience as we try to maintain the inner discipline
and moral integrity necessary for loving others. In this effort,
parents can learn a lot from people long involved in the civil
rights and women's liberation movements. In *Toward a New Psychology of Women*, Jean Baker Miller discusses women reconciling traditional and new attitudes, and what she says applies
to parenting as well: "There is no easy leaping over the only
system of thought and language that we have inherited. But we

are now becoming increasingly aware of the need for new assumptions and new words."

Why new assumptions and new words? There are two reasons: (1) because assumptions and words often affect the priorities we set for ourselves, in private as well as social life; and (2) because living in the midst of social change, in a time quite different from that of their parents and grandparents, parents, like artists, need a language and style appropriate to their responsibilities. George Orwell argued this point forty years ago in "Politics and the English Language." He wrote that "the present political chaos is connected with the decay of language, and ... one can probably bring about some improvement by starting at the verbal end." ̇

Learning a new language for parenting is especially necessary for fathers, it seems to me. For that reason, I devote this chapter to fatherhood and to the need for a careful, sometimes even radical, new understanding of how fathers must live if they are to fulfill the responsibilities of fatherhood at the present time.

Some of a father's choices, in his efforts to change, are painful ones. One of them involves taking more responsibility for tasks during the early stages of child-rearing that have been traditionally left to mothers. Having grown up expecting to work outside rather than inside the home, a man often takes on these responsibilities with reluctance and confusion, particularly if he has thought little about them before the child is born. And even his response to that event may come as something of a shock. Anxious about the birth of a child, but uncertain about the changes associated with his or her arrival, I was seldom fully conscious of a baby's presence until six months after the birth.

Women, by contrast, carry that knowledge early on; for some, morning sickness dramatizes the presence of a new being almost from the moment of conception. And by the time a baby is born, the mother has lived with a knowledge of new responsibilities — a radical presence — for some time.

Although I helped to care for the babies from the beginning — throwing my back out several times while rinsing diapers in the toilet — any full realization of their presence hit me only after about their sixth month. For that reason alone, I strongly recommend a prospective father's attending classes preparing him for the period of labor and delivery.

If a father is slow to learn how to care physically for the child, his ability to respond emotionally to him or her may prove even more difficult. Unskilled in the means of maintaining intimate relationships, particularly with males, he is seldom equipped to attend to a child's feelings in a manner that is essential to a father/son or father/daughter relationship. Traditionally, the skills necessary to make his way in the world ill equips a man for appreciating interdependency, and most of us learn interconnectedness only with effort. Any father anxious to have a more intimate relationship with his children than he had with his own father tries to correct this situation, with rewards for himself, but especially for his daughters and sons. As the number of men responsible for primary care of infants increases, so does our knowledge of how to go about this complicated, creative, frustrating, and enriching endeavor, as Dr. Kyle D. Pruett's research on the nurturing father suggests.

The choices a man must make, in this regard, have to do with self-understanding and self-definition (so recent commentators on the psychological and physical consequences of traditional male behavior seem to suggest). Nearing the end of the twentieth century, "many men find themselves on new and historically peculiar terrain," the psychologist Herbert J. Freudenberger has said. Their confusion has several sources, he argues, including new pressures for material success, changes in sexual stereotypes — with a shift in roles and rules — and the scarcity of acceptable mentors for them to emulate. A college senior, pointing to the fact that his parents accounted for five marriages between them, mentioned the increasing instability of marriages as another complicating factor about his own future.

Recent American poetry, drama, and fiction, in numerous portraits of the confused relationships between fathers and sons and between fathers and daughters, provide powerful evidence regarding the need for men to alter their ways of defining themselves. So frequently is this the case that Stanley Kunitz, who has received the Pulitzer Prize and numerous other awards for poetry, has spoken about "the mythic image of the absent father," someone who simply is not *there* because of death in war, abandonment, fatigue, or thoughtlessness. "Reduced to a number, a statistical integer, in the army or the factory or the marketplace," as Kunitz said, the father has frequently been unavailable to the son or daughter as a clear, much less a sustaining, presence.

In many cases, a father's absence is essentially physical and, therefore, explainable to the child: he died in Europe or the Pacific or Korea or Vietnam; his work, supporting and sustaining the family, makes it necessary for him to be gone for long periods of time; or he abandoned the children, leaving the mother or another relative to fulfill the responsibilities of both parents. In such cases, circumstances may define the absent father in a manner understandable or at least apparent to children.

In literature, the concept of the absent father concerns something more subtle, perhaps, in the long process of a child's making meaning of experience, particularly regarding his or her relationships with men. What do children come to expect of men through their experience with their fathers? And are traditional ways of being male an impediment to our own or our children's growth and development as mature and responsible beings in a democratic society? Are there ways of altering our behavior, as fathers, that might enable us to live and to encourage values in our children that would help them to expect and to build a more just society? These questions and others deserve serious thought when any father considers the kinds of social values he wishes to teach to his children.

SHARING HOUSEHOLD CHORES

Today many young men count on marrying a woman with a career, particularly as the prospects for well-paying jobs diminish and the cost of living increases. Reasonable, just, and necessary as it is for women to pursue careers of their own, this arrangement calls for careful planning.

Raised in homes in which women held full managerial responsibilities, newly married couples sometimes have a hard time adjusting psychologically to a new arrangement: Which one is responsible for cleaning? Which for cooking? Which for paying bills or keeping the car in shape? Raised in homes where women's roles were defined by tradition, rather than by choice, many men find it very difficult to negotiate these responsibilities; at the same time, some women refuse to recognize the wrenching effects on their husbands—some of whom are positively disposed to redefining themselves as husbands and fathers.

Two careers outside the home leave less time and energy for discussing even the simplest arrangements, particularly when couples decide to have children. As a member of a generation that faced such questions only later, after the children were nearly grown, I can only marvel at the relative success with which young mothers and fathers, including my own children, juggle the responsibilities associated with each of these decisions.

Once the child arrives, in spite of their strong commitment to being equal partners, men and women often return to traditional gender roles. In a declining economy, with the income of young families substantially less than it was a generation ago, husbands may spend longer hours at their work to earn extra money, while wives end up doing 80 percent of the child care and household chores.

At the same time, young husbands, comparing themselves with their fathers, may rightfully regard themselves as being more cooperative in doing household chores, while young wives, comparing their husbands' efforts with their own, remain dissatisfied with the disproportionate time they spend working in the home. In dealing with these conflicts, young mothers often turn to support groups, while young men, unused to expressing feelings of inadequacy—or admitting strains in sexual relations, another common complication—may not admit their confusion even to themselves. Thus do we, as fathers, perpetuate behavior that hinders our understanding of our own feelings and complicates our responding to our children's feelings as well.

Although most parents agree that the joy of having a child more than makes up for the difficulties associated with that task, mothers and fathers need the support of family, friends, a community, or even a counselor in sharing the responsibilities of parenthood. In a country where people move an average of once every five years, parents also spend a lot of time reorienting themselves in new environments so that they and their children have the benefit of a community, which is so essential to growth and development over a period of years.

EXPRESSING LOVE

A persistent theme in all discussions and dramatizations regarding "the difficulty of being male" is the search for and understanding of intimacy. A man's fear of losing control, and thus a preoccupation with power—a carry-over, apparently, from his manner of establishing a career—make intimacy difficult for him, not only with women, but also with other men.

This is obviously a very large subject, requiring more extensive discussion than I can provide here. But it is important enough and relevant enough to the teaching of values to address, even briefly. In doing so, I shall limit the discussion to the need for fathers to think seriously about their ways of expressing that most elemental concern, love. One can bungle many other aspects of child-rearing and still succeed, but any father failing to teach the several languages of love—through gesture, speech, and action—leaves a lot of repair work to be done by his children for the rest of their lives.

In approaching the subject of love, one recognizes, initially, how often it is relegated—in discussions of teaching values, as in most other discussions—to the periphery. However, love is such a common and persistent experience throughout life and so powerful an agent for personal growth and change, that it belongs, necessarily, at the forefront of any discussion of values. This is particularly true at this moment of history, when a rationalist mode of thinking about love dominates much of the discussion of development and behavior. Ethel Spector Person, a clinical psychologist who writes authoritatively and perceptively on the subject, has suggested, for example, that "the three great languages of contemporary Western culture—Christian, psychoanalytic, and Marxist—all conspire to devalue love."

Anyone doubting the accuracy of that statement might wish to compare the number of books on sex—books presenting techniques, instructions, statistical studies, moral exhortations—with the number written on love. To find an abundance of material on the latter subject, one must turn to the arts, poetry, fiction, and film — including the enormously popular gothic romances, written by and for women for the most part. But in the social sciences or in works focusing on patterns of human behavior (with all their how-to manuals), and certainly in most other academic disciplines, love enjoys only second- or third-class citizenship.

It is partially for this reason that I decided to make it central to this chapter; for without some understanding of the place of love, a central concept of nonviolence, few issues of justice and peace or of true citizenship make much sense. One of Martin Luther King's most powerful speeches, "Loving Your Enemies" (1957), for example, gave important advice seldom mentioned by proponents of political reform today. His goal, even in the midst of the most elemental struggle and conflict, was always reconciliation with his antagonist, which is possible only as long as loving one's enemy remains viable. Walt Whitman, a century ago, also pointed out that true democracy is impossible unless it is grounded in love between women and men, men and men, women and women; the same might be said of world citizenship.

Traditionally, in the education of children, women have been more attentive and direct about the importance of love; they have also been more responsible nurturers, listening closely to their children, and often speaking to them in their language. Since men, reflecting the values of the dominant culture, have traditionally regarded child-rearing as less central to their responsibilities, they need to give special thought and reflection to the meaning of fatherhood. This means taking seriously the evidence indicating that fathers have failed their sons and daughters in some basic sense, not out of willful neglect, necessarily, but out of habit or tradition, as well as a lack of imagination and insight into the implications of their behavior.

I say this out of great sympathy for what fathers must contend with in reorienting themselves to a rapidly changing world. Daily, a potentially damaging culture says to fathers in the late twentieth century, in subtle and not so subtle ways: "In facing the threat of nuclear war, inflation, and a declining economy, you are ineffectual: You do not earn enough money. Your efforts to care for your wife and children are inadequate and sometimes fruitless." To this indictment is added the feminist accusations: "Your habits and language are sexist. And whatever talent you bring to being a father is probably undermined by historical baggage you carry, including the influence of your father, uncles, grandfathers, and other male mentors."

Aware of such indictments, some of them justified, is it any wonder that many young men hesitate not only about becoming fathers, but also about marrying? Not surprisingly, they see lack of commitment "as a selfish but safer way to live," as Dr. Freudenberger has said. Much as I regret their decisions, I understand their uncertainties and anxieties, compounded by similar ones endured by young women, about how they should respond to traditional expectations and definitions of themselves.

Women over the past twenty years, however, have addressed their uncertainties and anxieties and have often developed communities around these concerns. Men, including many young men whom I teach, have been less successful in doing so.

For this and other reasons, it is wise for fathers—when they approach the subject of teaching values to their children—to consider anew the concept of manhood in both its sexual and ethical dimensions. Changing cultural patterns is not easy; it requires patience, understanding, and honesty on both sides. For although both sexes experience the pleasures and pains of love, their ways of defining and experiencing them differ significantly because of their cultural conditioning and psychological development. Such cultural conditioning affects not only our behavior, but also the way our children are treated or defined by others. Some fathers first become fully aware of the harmful effects of this conditioning through the experience of their own children.

My daughters, for example, have been helpful—and firm—in correcting my ignorance about issues peculiar to their own experience in growing up. Aware of the more obvious sexist traditions in our culture, I remained blind, nonetheless, to some of the subtler means of discrimination against women, until my daughters reached high school. That realization hit home the day my oldest daughter (later coordinator for health care for the homeless in a sizable city) informed me that a career counselor had told her that she had a choice, after graduation, of being a nurse or a secretary; having no objection to either, I was nonetheless incensed that her choices, unlike our sons', were arbitrarily circumscribed by such sexist "advising."

Both sexes, by general agreement, need "liberation" from stereotypes that limit or confine their development. In teaching values to their children, men, particularly, may find it necessary to resist a tendency to understand their task in terms of being a winner or loser in a power struggle. Teaching values in the home, as with many efforts in the public order, is a search for the truth, not the imposition of one ideology over another.

Similarly, a father upholds a set of values not as an absolute monarch, but as a teacher knowing that he may be ignored or resisted or rejected, initially. For this reason, he wisely overcomes a temptation to insist that his love is dependent upon the child's obeying "laws" or merely parroting opinions learned from him. In one of his letters to the early Christians, St. Paul counseled fathers against nagging their children, lest they become disheartened. (The problem of the stern, impatient father has apparently been around for a while.)

In the early years, yes, one has to insist at times upon absolute obedience, particularly in values related to the safety and civility of the child: "Don't run into the street. Don't play with matches. Say 'please' and 'thank you.' "

By the time children go to school, however, they, unlike the man in Robert Frost's "Mending Wall" (who repeats his father's adage that "good fences make good neighbors"), are less inclined merely to repeat their father's sayings. Rather, like the thinking beings they are, children begin asking pertinent questions, such as "*Why* do fences make good neighbors?" Before long, and for a variety of reasons, they begin challenging these sayings: "Before I built a wall I'd ask to know / What I was walling in or walling out. / And to whom I was like to give offense." As teachers of values, parents need to have a variety of negotiating skills at their disposal—they need to know when to be firm and when to relent in insisting upon the values they regard as essential to their children's welfare.

LISTENING CAREFULLY, PROVIDING REASSURANCE

A father needs to give reasons for insisting upon one set of values over another and, if possible, should suggest how those values relate to his general concern, his love, for his son or daughter. Such reassurances are communicated, obviously, not merely by embraces and words, but also by deeds, particularly through the husband's behavior toward his wife, toward other children, and toward outsiders as well.

Once after I had disciplined his younger brother, for example, my oldest son watched me sullenly, with tears welling in his eyes. "That's not fair," he said firmly to me. "You shouldn't have treated him that way. He didn't do anything wrong." And my older son was right, of course. I had reacted more out of frustration than anything else, at the end of the day. It was easier just to shout at one offender for misbehaving and to send him to his room than to take on the role of prosecutor, judge, and jury, in mediating a conflict among the children.

As the children grew older, I improved, perhaps, in my ability to talk with them and to communicate what I thought and how I wished them to behave, without relying on power plays of this kind. Or maybe, as they came to tower over me, I simply realized that the old strategies wouldn't work anyway.

In the teenage years, a natural time of rebellion, as children try on or try throwing out their parents' values, they sometimes put us to the fiercest tests. A high-school girl, for example, reasoning (falsely, I think) that her father put too much emphasis upon formal education, dropped out of school. Concerned as he was, he tried, instead of increasing the pressure on her to stay, to offer several choices, alternatives, one of which she eventually selected. Had he been adamant about her remaining in the high school where she was, she might well have chucked the whole enterprise. As it was, she moved to a different high school, where she became a member of the National Honor Society, and went on to college.

Born with divining rods to probe our weakest points, teenagers seem to delight in jumping up and down on them, to test our mettle. So a father, while holding firm to his own values, must convey in whatever way possible his confidence in a son's or daughter's right to choose and to live by his or her own values as well.

In this complicated process of communicating with children, and other elemental aspects of child-rearing, women are often at once more imaginative and more concrete, as I suggested earlier. By that I mean that they usually understand the close relationship between love and the teaching of values and manage to convey those subtleties to children. Perhaps the first requirement of "relearning fatherhood" begins here, with men making a disciplined effort to appreciate that relationship. To do so, fathers need to become active listeners and responders in teaching children at every age, as women often do, and with greater care and patience.

Does anything demand more intelligence and imagination, in fact, than talking to several children at various ages, at the same time, with that persistent attentiveness to needs and desires, fears and hopes, of the moment? And have not women been more adept at this skill than men? Without wanting to suggest that love is communicated primarily or most effectively by language, I do think it is a key factor in conveying to children a sense of their importance and of other values as well. A willingness to spend time talking and reading to children is central to the whole process of communicating what is important to us, as parents. For most men, this requires a conscious choice to focus their attention, to "be there," rather than merely to tolerate the child's questions, comments, and responses.

Women's common complaint that men seldom listen or respond when spoken to has implications regarding fathers' relationships to children as well. So it is well for men to make a conscious effort to recognize the importance of verbal communication during the early life of a child. Nothing dramatizes the importance of such communication better than focusing one's attention on a baby in the first months, and watching its response to speech. In some infants, one can literally see their souls stretch and awaken at the sound of the human voice.

As a young father, I had no trouble talking to the children when they were babies; the real test came once they began to talk, some with lengthy and complicated stories about the day's events. At that point, I found myself retreating to my work; one of my sons reminds me still of the time I took him to a Boston Red Sox's game, only to haul out a book, reading rather than simply attending to events that were important to him. Later, I learned the value of having friends with interests different from my own (and closer to my children's); those friends taught them, for instance, to do woodworking and to fish.

Although women sometimes resent the suggestion that they are innately more attentive to children than men, it is difficult for us, sometimes, to think otherwise. Whether their parenting skills are the result of psychological development or cultural conditions or some other process, women often appear to communicate with children more effectively, more "naturally." Isn't the native language referred to as "the mother tongue," after all?

Whatever the case, for both women and men, being a parent inevitably calls for some reflection on the practice of the art of communicating with children. It calls for applying what one learns as naturally as possible — that is, not forgetting to be oneself, as the author of *P.E.T. Parent Effectiveness Training* suggests — yet developing new and compensatory skills within the context of being a parent.

STAYING IN TOUCH

In being a parent, as I said earlier, one can fail at many aspects of the task and still rear children who become responsible, imaginative, affectionate adults. Failing them at one age, one often has a chance to make up for that later on. A young father preoccupied with his career and more "important" matters when his children are two and four may have no time to read to them or to listen carefully to their questions and projects. By the time they are eight and ten, he may learn, with luck, just how "important" their times together are not only for his children, but also for him. In parenting, as in many other things, one learns that failing the first time does not rule out making up and even succeeding later on.

Understanding fatherhood also means giving serious thought to how one will sustain close touch with his children as they grow and mature. It is an on-going process, a life-long effort, with possibilities for refinement and improvement along the way. I write this, remembering my last conversation with my father. Weak and confused from a fall and — although I did not suspect it at the time — in his last hours, he said again what he had always said at the end of our weekly phone conversations over the years: "Be sure to tell all your family that we love them."

Finally, as one wise veteran, grandfather of ten, reminded me—when six of ours were teenagers *all at once*—even the most graceless duckling sometimes acquires grace later on. Children who seem destined to be thoughtless, insensitive, self-centered beasts at sixteen, with care and tending and a lot of patience often grow into generous, compassionate beings at twenty-four. Prayer and someone else's love sometimes work wonders, so one must not take the whole burden or responsibility on oneself.

Although this discussion about values focuses primarily on the family, it has implications for the wider community, where priorities must be altered and traditional values reexamined for the benefit of all. Understanding fatherhood means understanding power relationships between adults and children; it also means appreciating our significance as father figures to other children. The models we carry in our heads, the authority figures we remember and emulate in our daily lives, influence the way we define and understand the concept of authority, generally, in government, education, and religion. Democracy in the wider culture, like almost everything else, depends in part upon an individual's understanding and experience of it at a mother's *and* a father's knee.

5

GROWING INTO FAITH

Peace among the religions is the prerequisite for peace among the nations.

— Hans Küng
Theology for the Third Millennium

Wherever people seek the good, justice, humanitarian love, solidarity, communion and understanding between people, ... the resurrected one is present, because the cause for which he lived, suffered, was tried and executed is being carried forward.

— Leonardo Boff
Jesus Christ Liberator

How does a parent convey to a child the essential sacredness of life? How does one suggest, in as many ways as possible, the profound mystery at the heart of all things human? How can I say to my children and grandchildren that, though often episodic, confusing, even painful, life is an opportunity to be treasured, to be grateful for, to be seized and relished for what it offers? How might I say to them what I once wrote to other young people in a brief verse entitled "Syllabus"?

> You will teach me, first, my students,
> the character of my indifference
> and the dark confusion of being young.

61

> I will teach you then, my students,
> a hope that lies beneath the surface,
> a love inherent in the nature of things.
> Follow the course of it to the end of knowing;
> gather the thread of it line by line.

As parents, we convey a positive attitude regarding the essential mystery of life in many ways, particularly if a long life enables us to be with and to talk with our children at various stages of their lives. Often too inexperienced or too "busy" when our children are young to discuss our own sense of God or gods or transcendence, we may eventually do so as they approach adolescence or adulthood.

RELIGIOUS AWE, A SENSE OF WONDER

A learned man, in his late sixties, once told me about an important childhood event during which his father conveyed a vivid sense of life's sacredness to him. On a visit to the Rocky Mountains when he was eight years old, he and his father watched silently as the sun rose and colored the vast stretch of land before them. The presence of such power and beauty, shared by the two of them, has remained with the man ever since; and that feeling of religious awe, experienced sixty years ago, has been kept alive, in part, through his effort to communicate it to his children and grandchildren.

Most children are born, fortunately, with a religious sense of life. Henry Vaughan, a seventeenth-century English poet, remembered early childhood ("those early days! when I / Shin'd in my Angell-infancy") as a time of meditation upon and endless delight in creation:

> When on some gilded Cloud, or flower
> My gazing soul would dwell an hour . . .
> [And I] felt through all this fleshly dress
> Bright shoots of everlastingness.

Two centuries later, in "Ode: Intimations of Immortality from Recollections of Early Childhood," William Wordsworth described his own early life as a period bathed in the light of heaven:

> There was a time when meadow, grove, and
>   stream,
> The earth, and every common sight,
>   To me did seem
> Appareled in celestial light.

In a brief poem written in the first grade, one of our daughters expressed her delight in the universe in this way: "Animals in the woods. Happy Birthday Everything!"

As long as parents provide a loving environment—plain and tasty food, pleasant surroundings, and some security—most children respond to questions about the value of life with an everlasting Yes! During the early years, particularly between the ages of one and five, one sees it in their eyes, when, in moments of self-forgetfulness, they literally become whatever catches their attention: a bird hopping across the grass, a cat climbing a tree, a child whom they have never seen before entering a room or walking up to them in the park. Such responses resemble what has been called "first order religious language"; they are similar to those spontaneous utterances of awe and joy by saints and mystics in acknowledging the unity of all living things.

ELEMENTAL QUESTIONS

As they grow a bit older, attend school, and gain more experience—as they first endure physical pain or personal injustice at the hands of others or as they learn about death—children begin asking complicated questions, with powerful religious implications. And how uneasy they can make us feel: Where do people go when they die? Why does God let some people starve while others have more food than they need? Why do we build weapons that could kill children and animals and trees and flowers everywhere in the world?

At such times, in the midst of other chores, a mother or father may be tempted simply to repeat the wisdom of that old gospel hymn "Farther Along": "Tempted and tried, we're oft' made to wonder / Why it should be thus all the day long?" Regarding a child's questions, however, a parent must try to respond as honestly as possible, listening carefully and deciding how general or how specific he or she needs to be. In discussing religious values, a mother or father listens not so much to what the child says as to what he or she means; through these dialogues, as well as through prayer, liturgy, and other religious practices, abstract concepts become concrete.

All questions about elemental matters of life and death—all matters of ultimate concern—are "religious," to some degree, and influence how a child—and later an adult—understands matters of faith. Although this is not the place for an extended discussion of spirituality, or of particular religious traditions, I do want to say a few things about helping children develop a religious sense of themselves and the world around them. Very few of the concepts I discuss in this book, in fact, have much meaning or usefulness if one regards them as mere "techniques" apart from their philosophical or religious grounding in human experience.

Each religious tradition provides meaningful rituals for communicating a sense of wonder about the majesty and mystery of life, many of them linked to important events in life. The Quaker tradition—as Elise Boulding, sociologist, peacemaker, and grandmother, explains—uses silence "to introduce all kinds of special occasions, from meals to family celebrations." She goes so far as to say, in fact, that parents can fulfill their vocation as parents only if they "make themselves receptive to a daily inflowing of divine love." Many parents from other denominations would agree. What is said on such occasions—prayers at mealtime or bedtime or on important celebrations—is perhaps less important than the fact that parents and children express their gratitude or longing or sorrow or joy *together*, formally or informally.

Twenty years ago, for example, in an effort to offer a positive alternative to what they regarded as a negative religious environment, several local families initiated a weekly liturgy that was held in homes, parks, and community centers. Improvised (and occasionally disorganized), the Floating Parish—and similar experiments elsewhere in the country—tried to reflect the values and reforms associated with Vatican II and the ecumenical movement. As an experiment, it indicated the adults' willingness to assume responsibility for their children's religious education and to make the links between religious belief and practice, between moral values and nonviolent social change. In Latin America, at about the same time, the base communities began to bring ordinary people together to explore the connections between the experience of people in the Old and New Testaments and themselves. In order to make children aware of the best in various religious traditions, other parents have committed themselves to similar "homemade" efforts in religious education, particularly if "the institution"—churches, synagogues, or mosques—in their area fails to do so.

The presence of God, or an awareness of transcendence in human history, informs every religious denomination and tradition, and parents can help children to remain open to the possibility of that presence in their daily lives. When the children are young, parents can do this through family practices such as prayer before meals or at bedtime; discussions and meditation, however random or occasional; or simply "quiet time" in the midst of the hustle and bustle of contemporary family life.

Encouraging a kind of awe and gratitude before the beauty and resilience of human beings, plants, animals, and natural phenomena takes time; it involves "being with" children, rather than just instructing or lecturing them. Rachel Carson, one of the great environmentalists in recent American history, often spoke and wrote about the importance of encouraging young people's delight in the universe. In *The Sense of Wonder*, for example, she described how important her young nephew was in teaching her about the excitement and mystery of the sea, plant life, lightning, birds, and animals. In the midst of a busy career, as editor-in-chief of publications for the U.S. Fish and Wildlife Service and, later, as a writer, she took time to explore the coast of Maine with him. If a child is to keep alive his sense of wonder, Carson said, "he needs the companionship of at least one adult who can share it, rediscovering with him the joy, excitement and mystery of the world we live in."

Parents may feel inadequate, however, when confronted with the "eager, sensitive mind of a child and a world of complex physical nature," Carson wrote. Parents may think they cannot possibly instruct their children on subjects they know little about themselves. In such efforts, "it is not half so important to *know* as to *feel*," however, for "if facts are the seeds that later produce knowledge and wisdom, then the emotions and the impressions are the fertile soil in which the seeds must grow."

What Carson said about encouraging a sense of wonder applies equally well to religious faith. Long accustomed to associating religion primarily with belief rather than practice, with theology rather than with faith, with doctrine rather than with persons, we may be ill prepared to nurture a religious sensibility in our children. But there are positive things that can be done in extending the boundaries of our definition of religion and in allowing our children to understand religion more fully and to define it more accurately.

In addressing questions of a religious nature, parents must allow, at the same time, for a wide range of responses from children. In these matters, as in all areas of teaching values, an attentive parent keeps in mind children's way of making religious meaning of major events in their young lives; this is obviously less difficult when responding to their "positive" encounter with awe and wonder than when responding to their "negative" encounter with violence and injustice, both of which may lead them to reflect upon the meaning of life.

The death of a classmate or a grandparent, for example, may provoke strong, sometimes unexpected reactions: denial, first; then anger; then unexpected crying; perhaps indifference, then inordinate questioning—all perfectly understandable reactions for a child, or anyone else. On occasion, these responses come in rapid succession.

Children's responses to the threat of violence, similarly, including their fears about nuclear war, may depend upon what they observe in their parents' reactions. Does the mother express or suppress feeling? Does the father imply that it is natural to cry, for example, or to respond in some other way when events or anxieties affect him deeply?

Recent historical events, particularly since the United States first used weapons of mass destruction in Hiroshima and Nagasaki, have further complicated the teaching of religious values to children, as well as the religious attitudes of adults. According to recent research by the International Physicians for Social Responsibility, for example, many children grow up terribly anxious about the future. A parent's ignoring these fears makes children feel less rather than more secure, since the children may regard a mother's or a father's failure to do anything about the threat of nuclear war as a sign of their parents not caring about them. A parent's taking political action, on the other hand, gives children a sense that perhaps the danger can be overcome; it enables them to retain some hope for the future, in spite of present dangers.

Incorporating relevant facts about the arms race and predictions about a nuclear war obviously complicates the effort of any parent who wishes to encourage a religious sense of the world. Such elemental matters raise basic questions about our own religious faith, as well as the lives and religious sensibilities of our children, including: (1) Do we need to do some serious thinking, ourselves, about essential matters of life and death? (2) How prepared are we to deal with such questions within the confines of traditional religious teachings? and (3) What choices might we make available to our children, from the religious traditions we know, as they try to understand and to confront the basic religious questions posed by life in a nuclear age? That is, what aspects of our own tradition are honestly meaningful to us as we try to make meaning of our lives at this moment in history?

RELIGIOUS INSTITUTIONS

For many parents, programs in religious education at a church or synagogue are an essential aid in teaching basic religious values to children, particularly when such programs build upon the social teachings of the tradition: Old and New Testament readings on peace, justice, and the care of orphans and widows; papal encyclicals such as *Pacem in Terris*; pastoral letters and resolutions on nuclear disarmament by several Christian denominations; the statements by other religious bodies on poverty, homelessness, war, human rights, and protecting the environment. Among the ones I am familiar with, materials for children published by the Unitarian/Universalist and United Christian Congregational churches are particularly impressive; so are the various manuals of a more directly practical nature, on teaching nonviolence through cooperative games and global awareness, published by Educators for Social Responsibility.

In our own family and among families closest to us while our children were growing up, we were very uncertain about how we could make the social teachings of the church, in our case social encyclicals and pastoral letters since Vatican II, accessible to our children. Most religious education programs ignored them at that time; and even when people on the church payroll talked about values related to peace and justice, the context was a top-down management institution. In addition, the so-called religious message generally implied a Jansenistic hatred of the body and little respect for women.

Positive responses to this dilemma in the Christian church are offered by various ecumenical and/or interfaith experiments, including the Community of the Living Spirit, in Wisconsin; the Newman Centers at large Midwestern and Southwestern state universities; St. Stephen's Parish in Minneapolis; and so on. Less circumscribed by yet still dependent upon the institutional church, they keep social justice concerns at the center of their liturgies and activities.

For the past twenty years, any parent's attempt to pass along—to recommend and to criticize—a religious tradition has been complicated also by people's alienation from or at least a general indifference to the institutional church. New awakenings, symbolized by the powerful currents associated with liberation theology and by reforms within various Jewish, Catholic, and Orthodox groups and Protestant denominations, have altered the way many people understand and practice their faith.

In the midst of such changes, parents are being asked to learn a new religious language and at the same time to communicate with children unfamiliar with what went before. Is it any wonder that conscientious parents often feel, as a father of four said recently, that "we don't know what we are doing."

Many parents reared and educated within an institutional church soon discover that their children have little use for traditional—or, for us, conventionally defined—beliefs and practices, even if the parents rely on the institution for ceremonies at the time of marriage, the birth of their children, or the death of a family member. Few children of our close friends—many of them educated in Catholic schools from kindergarten through undergraduate, graduate, and professional training—regularly attend Sunday services, for example. Such a shift in priorities not only places the burden of religious education almost totally on the parents; it also makes them feel as if they have failed in the moral education of their children.

Friends of ours, devout Catholics and parents of six grown children, speak periodically about their children not carrying on the family religious practices, as they had hoped. Yet a closer look at the lives of those children, now in their thirties, indicates that the parents were extraordinarily successful in conveying to them a sense of the sacredness of life, the value of persons, and the sustaining quality of faith. All of their children have chosen vocations among the helping services; several have worked in Africa and Central America in the Peace Corps and similar agencies, and others rear orphans from abroad as members of their own families. Although most of them, in other words, do not live the "religious" life as it was previously defined, they live lives informed by values traditionally associated with religious faith, even as they limit their association with the institutional church to being married and having their infant children baptized by ordained clergy. In various ways, that is, many Christians and Jews simply understand and apply the basic teachings of their faith in a manner quite different from their elders and even from their younger selves.

In a nuclear age, traditional teachings regarding the morality of the just war, for example, are irrelevant to many religious people. While interesting historically, the Augustinian requirements for conducting a just war make little sense in a nuclear age. For women, sexist practices or pronouncements, such as the Pauline counsel that wives should be subject to their husbands, seriously undermine the applicability of much theological writing. For others, certain Old Testament writings—such as the statement in Genesis encouraging men and women to "be fruitful and multiply, and fill the earth and subdue it; and have dominion ... over every living thing that moves upon the earth" — appear to conflict directly with the wise counsel of others calling us to responsible stewardship of the earth.

In this century, much of the moral leadership in social justice, in fact, appears to have come from people — Bertrand Russell, Albert Einstein, Hannah Arendt, for example — who derived their understanding of moral responsibility not from "religion," as it is traditionally understood, but from ethical standards about being a good neighbor to the earth and all its people. Stanley Kunitz, in a remark about his own spiritual life, suggests this contemporary perspective: "I have no religion — perhaps that is why I think so much about God." For conventionally "religious" writers, as well, whoever is in charge of the universe remains rather unaccountable, as if responsibility for the present state of affairs rests pretty much in human hands.

Almost all those associated with nonviolent movements for social change, nonetheless, have emphasized the spiritual roots of their social commitment, and several of them — such as Gandhi, Dorothy Day, Thomas Merton, Daniel and Philip Berrigan, Oscar Romero, and Martin Luther King — have written extensively on that topic. For that reason, biographies of these people, as well as selections of their own writings, are useful aids in helping children "grow into faith."

Many remarkable figures in "conventional" religious history have also been proponents of peacemaking, friendship with the earth, and nonviolent resistance to injustice. Examples include Saints Stanislaus and Greb, Francis of Assisi, and Thomas More, as well as the three great religious figures described by Ammon Hennacy in his famous saying: "Love without courage and wisdom is sentimentality, as with the ordinary church member. Courage without love and wisdom is foolhardiness, as with the ordinary soldier. Wisdom without love and courage is cowardice, as with the ordinary intellectual. Therefore, one who has love, courage, and wisdom is one in a million, who moves the world, as with Jesus, Buddha, and Gandhi."

In teaching values to children, it is essential for us to define "religion" in a manner much broader than has traditionally been the case in institutional religion. For young people, particularly, that means concentrating on primary religious language — a sense of the sacred, prayer, love, repentance, transcendence, and reconciliation—rather than on secondary religious language associated with theology and systematic thought.

Our children and grandchildren live out the implications of our own beliefs, responding to "the signs of the times," but often in ways we do not understand. In the United States, particularly, young people are even more aware than we are of the implications of pluralistic society, including the plurality of religions and theologies. Growing up in a world where the churches themselves foster new awareness and appreciation of one another and encourage new ways of relating to Hindus, Muslims, Native Americans, and Confucians, as well as to crosscultural and feminist perspectives, children sometimes teach us a lot about growing into religious faith. At the same time, parents are wise to maintain religious beliefs and practices that enable children to mediate between traditional and nontraditional ways of being religious. In doing so, they acquaint young people with the collective wisdom of the major religious traditions of the world, including the most ancient ones that have survived the centuries and that continue to inform the great civilizations of the Middle and Far East.

Having few clearly defined communities that they can lean on for help in teaching values to the children, and lacking a clearly defined body of knowledge and forms, parents sometimes find their job of encouraging religious values enormously complicated. Unhappy with the old, they sometimes have few viable or well-defined alternatives. In recent years, the available ones have sometimes been the ones parents created for themselves —for instance, cooperative religious education programs independent of the institutional church or synagogue. At times, "secular" schools and activities where social values are communicated and encouraged by the people involved do a better job of emphasizing the importance of religious faith than churches do.

Our present dilemma about "what is to be done," sometimes understood as the conflict between "religion" and "faith," may lead to considerable misunderstanding regarding basic religious concepts, images, and forms. As a result, our religious discussions—our quests for meaning—are often marked by intensity, anxiety, even anger, with accusations of "hypocrisy" or "heresy" on all sides. So-called traditionalists seem, at times, unable to distinguish between religion and faith, assuming that both refer to the same human need; so-called critics, on the other hand, sometimes show only limited knowledge of or respect for saints and reformers and apostles who went before. As a consequence, the profound religious experience of men and women throughout the world is disregarded, in a way that does not do justice to the region, the culture, or the people involved.

RELIGIOUS LANGUAGE

As language fails the churches, it also fails us in our efforts to explain to our children what once appeared to be "simple truths." At such a time, we need to try to recover basic concepts—or perhaps to name them more precisely—if we are to understand them within the context of our own lives.

Some adults ask with alarm, for example: "Whatever happened to the word *sin*?" For centuries the term seemed to "name" people's encounter with evil in the world. Is such a term useful any more? Has its appropriation by institutions and churches, to cover everything from sexual promiscuity to the wanton murder of thousands, so discredited the term that it is no longer useful in human discourse? Or is *sin* perhaps still appropriate in naming the hindrances to life, liberty, and the pursuit of happiness endured by many people throughout the world? Is it accurate to call wasting money, talent, and natural resources on nuclear weapons a "sin" against the poor of the world? And aren't most traditional "sins" inconsequential before the horrors of mass genocide and exploitation that characterize the behavior of those in power in recent history? How else can we regard the monumental evils of secret wars, spying, and violence against innocent people and the environment? In honesty, we have to admit that these are often the inevitable consequences of economic and political decisions made by rich and powerful minorities, sometimes including ourselves.

I approach the topic of religious language by posing these questions; like many parents, I am uncertain about the answers and about my own way of dealing with the questions. My experience and intuitions suggest, however, that encouraging a religious sensibility in children obligates me to pose honest questions rather than to pretend I have the answers, particularly as my children moved into adolescence and postadolescence. I have seen too many young people alienated by those who employ an "answer man" approach to religion. Institutions have a tendency to behave that way, and perhaps perpetuate themselves by doing so; thus do they treat doctrine and belief more seriously than they treat people and faith.

For several reasons, parents, since they are forever parents, need to develop a subtler, more sophisticated way of responding and relating to their children about religious matters. First, religious discussions between parents and children in any age reflect the tension between past experience and present-day knowledge. Over a century ago, John Henry Newman, in *Essay on the Development of Christian Doctrine* (1845), pointed to the gradual unfolding of our understanding of the teachings of Jesus; and subsequent historical scholarship regarding the role of women in the early church—and the doctrine of "the just war"—suggests the danger of regarding religious truths as fixed or unchanging. In light of these considerations, parents may wonder how they can be authentic, as religious persons and teachers, when their own understanding of what is truly religious is always developing, changing, in many instances extending the boundaries of faith.

Second, religious pluralism is a significant fact about the world our children will move into, and a respect for their capacity to grow in faith means conveying a sense of traditions other than our own. In educating children, particularly beyond the early years, parents do little harm and perhaps much good by acknowledging uncertainties and inadequate knowledge about their own religious tradition as well as by showing appreciation for the richness and wisdom of other traditions.

In the United States, Native American religions, for example, have much wisdom to offer in our quest for the meaning of life and our relationship to the earth. Their myths and stories are among the great repositories of religious teaching about the environment and our responsibilities to it, as this representative prayer of Black Elk suggests: "Grandmother Earth, hear me! . . . The two-leggeds, the four-leggeds, the wingeds, and all that move upon You are Your children. With all beings and all things we shall be as relatives; just as we are related to You, O Mother."

So a knowledge and understanding of such lore may be crucial to decisions we make about the future. Learning about native American culture is not a mere indulgence in antiquarianism; it reflects a respect for one aspect of our history and culture that has been relegated to a secondary place in American education. The rush to assert and to perpetuate the so-called Western tradition has some value, also, but may have less bearing on the present dilemma than religious traditions native to our own land.

WORLD RELIGIONS

How primitive people lived in the face of uncertainty and danger often speaks to the times. At no period in history, perhaps, has there been such a need to understand and to appreciate the rich, detailed variety of religious history. In this effort, the experience of missionaries and disinterested scholars — anthropologists and cultural historians — is invaluable for the education of our children.

Such people have gone not as conquerors or exploiters or even as bearers of "the truth" to "pagans," as was often true among earlier missionaries and explorers, but rather as witnesses to the lives and struggles of people in Asia, Africa, and the islands of the Pacific — people who, in the rush of events, are now our neighbors. In learning about these cultures, we may become aware of the suffering imposed upon them by earlier explorers and colonizers, as well as the careless destruction of their environment by the so-called developed countries, and their manner of surviving in spite of that. Today, we all share the effects of rampant industrialization, and together we must try to dissipate some of its worst consequences.

Appreciating the infinite richness of people's religious experience, I have suggested, is central to our regaining a deep reverence for life and conveying that to our children. For "it is not entirely foolish to suggest that the rise of the concept of 'religion' is in some ways correlated with a decline in the practice of religion itself," Wilfred Cantwell Smith once said.

Many people, obviously, continue to regard the traditional religions of the West as satisfactory guides to understanding the meaning of life; but increasing numbers of people, particularly since World War II, do not. The age, in fact, is sometimes characterized as a random search for systems that satisfy humankind's deepest longing for an understanding and appreciation of the sacred, for a new understanding of the source of creation. Feminist theology, for example, has reminded us of the limitations imposed upon "God" by patriarchal views inherited from both Judaism and Christianity. And liberation theology has suggested the limitations of the philosophical or reified understandings of Christianity that have dominated religious discussion over the past century.

"If we are to go beyond [our present problems]," Noam Chomsky has said, "our work must be guided by a vision of a future that is attainable and worth achieving and it must be part of a sustained and long-term commitment by many people ... who share this vision." Such visions inevitably depend upon people's sense of what life is for and how it should be lived, and upon their experience in knowing, willing, and feeling.

Teaching values to our children means addressing the crisis of faith posed by a nuclear threat and trying to heal the spiritual wounds resulting from this moral confusion, as well as from discrimination, poverty, oppression, war, and pollution. In doing so, parents may find themselves drawing upon the rich resources of various traditions and sometimes challenging the dehumanizing implications of the religious institutions with which they have been closely associated.

Richard McBrien, a regular columnist for Catholic periodicals, a priest and a teacher at the University of Notre Dame, once encouraged such a clarification of thought in a memorable reflection on the questions, "What if there were a nuclear holocaust that left no churches, altars, seminaries, bishops, books, not even a bible? What hopes and aspiration will [people] have for themselves and for what is left of humankind? What sense of responsibility will they have for the rebuilding of the earth?"

Acknowledging the peculiarity of his manner of posing these issues, Father McBrien used the questions for a good purpose, concluding with a simple statement about the primary task of the church — and, one might say, of parents wishing to encourage a strong commitment to religious principles in their children. "The primary task," he said, "would be the nurturing of a way of life based on love (John 15:12)." If that principle is established, the other values compatible with most of the major religions of the world will follow. Without it — and perhaps even with it — lecturing, law-giving, and top-down management are a waste of time and energy.

Langdon Gilkey, a contemporary theologian, understands religious people's movement away from the institutional church and the requirements of faith — as well as the need to "defend" them — as a rediscovery of the obligation to love. Such a change is compatible with the manner of recommending values to our children that I have mentioned thus far. Uneasy with both the ethical relativism of the wider culture and the moral absolutism of what Lawrence Kohlberg called the hardliner's "bag of virtues," we try to navigate the "middle way" of encouraging our children to grow into faith, respectful yet critical of previous styles of being religious.

PART III

AUTHENTIC WAYS OF DOING

6

RELEARNING PATRIOTISM

The more experience one has with [the world's] children,
the more one appreciates how pervasive nationalism is as
an instrument of ego.

> — Robert Coles
> *The Political Life of Children*

The love of one's country is a splendid thing, but why
should love stop at the border?

> — Pablo Casals

Any close observer of children recognizes that they have a
political life. As Dr. Robert Coles, after thousands of interviews
with children, has argued: We learn our politics, as well as language
and religion, at our parents' knees. At an early age, children
develop a sense, in imitation of their parents, of who has
power over whom and how they use it. During their first days
at school, their instinct for survival enables them to negotiate
their way among various, sometimes conflicting, influences —
parents, teachers, and playmates. Early on, they begin to learn
how society works and whom they can trust. Being treated with
respect at home, they will expect similar courtesies at school and
in the community.

In children's minds, struggling always to make meaning of
experience, symbols associated with their native country provide
ways of shaping and asserting a personality. And a nation's slo-

gans and history—"America the beautiful" or "Don't tread on me" or "We're no. 1"—become elementally associated with young people's understanding of themselves as human beings.

What children make of nationality and what parents encourage them to make of it, as Anna Freud and others have suggested, are abiding influences on how children (and, later, adults) define themselves as citizens. So a father's deciding whether he will buy war toys for his children or not deserves more than casual consideration. Giving children miniature rifles, tanks, and bazookas with "play" bullets tells them that resorting to violence and killing is an acceptable mode of behavior.

Similarly, being subjected to a steady diet of Rambo movies or prejudiced remarks about "the others," children may come to regard "the others"—Russians or Chinese or Vietnamese or Iraqis or whomever the state defines as enemies at the moment —as less good, less human than themselves.

Being read stories about or meeting people from those countries, on the other hand, may lead children to identify themselves with "the others." And a conscious effort by parents to broaden their children's experience of races and beliefs different from their own challenges their sometimes narrow "reading" of reality and their chauvinist attitude toward the world's nations and peoples.

All nations have ways of perpetuating beliefs and attitudes on a wide range of ethical issues, and of getting succeeding generations to accept policies that reflect a country's view of itself. In previous ages, the work of the state was done through word of mouth or history books and newspapers; in our time, videos and television perform that task with inordinate speed and efficiency, not through words, but through powerful electronic images. The media provide a structure, as Dr. Coles has said, on which we "hang a range of oughts, noughts, maybes, ifs."

Through their teaching of values, however, parents still have some control concerning which national myths or traditions will receive priority in their homes—those enthroning violence and competition, or others emphasizing nonviolence and cooperation.

Resisting images—and, by implication, values—of the dominant culture takes some effort, however, since it involves asking a child, at times, to be "different" from his or her contemporaries. Not knowing the latest jingle about Marlboro cigarettes or McDonald's makes children feel "out of it," perhaps, with their classmates and contemporaries; however, being "out of it" may also keep their minds less cluttered with dross and their imaginations more accessible to their own creations.

In upholding values quite different from those being dished out by the media, parents may wonder why the struggle to live responsibly, for the common good, seems so relentless. Living in a culture that promises and often provides so many desirable things, we are often unprepared for the conflicts and disappointments that an adherence to humane values evokes. To whom should we pledge our allegiance, for example: To presidents who give the orders to invade Panama, to mine the harbors of Nicaragua, or to bomb Libya? Or to the ordinary people of Panama, Nicaragua, or Libya, as well as to the young American soldiers who die as a result of these orders? Loyal to our country, and concerned about the consequences of public policy for our children and our grandchildren, we may feel very much in conflict with ourselves, as well as with our leaders; we may long for a new way of doing things and a new language for naming them.

Perhaps I can best illustrate need for a new language by reference to one concept, patriotism. In speaking of patriotism or nationalism, we confront one of our real dilemmas as teachers of values in an imperial culture, since patriotism affects the mental development of children in many ways. In negotiating our way among conflicting values in modern life, how can we possibly communicate the significance of patriotism to our children? Is the concept so discredited, in fact, that one should not treat it seriously at all?

Is it possible even to use this word, *patriotism,* without calling up almost every oversimplification and form of ignorance that has contributed to our present misunderstanding of the term? In political cartoons, the image of the citizen-patriot has become a caricature: someone standing on a street corner waving a flag, calling people names, and justifying the worst cruelties and injustices of American interventionism and greed. He or she has replaced the anarchist of the early twentieth century, with gritted teeth and bomb in hand, as a subject of satire.

But I see no reason to surrender the term *patriotism* to those who use it to justify bombing and pillaging the rest of the world by the United States. Patriotism carries with it an inheritance, a legacy, of loving, supporting, and defending one's home. What we need to do, really, is to try to understand those noble inclinations within the circumstances of the present.

In saying this, I realize that patriotism would now best be understood as a commitment to dissent that would keep us out of war, rather than justify our wading into it. Aren't the most patriotic persons in the United States those who keep us not only from dying in a nuclear war, but also from waging it in the first place? Almost every American recognized that the Chinese students protesting government corruption and a lack of free speech during the late spring of 1989 acted in the best interests of their country. Suppliant and nonviolent in addressing the party leadership, in rallies at Tiananmen Square in Beijing and in eighty major cities throughout China, they won the hearts and minds of people throughout the world. Yet how many Americans recognize the equally patriotic impulses of Americans acting to halt the manufacture of the MX missile or the stealth bomber, so destructive to our economy and our environment?

A NEW UNDERSTANDING OF PATRIOTISM

If, as I am suggesting, the old patriotism won't do, what will the new patriotism look like? What will characterize the person guided by the social values attendant to the signs of the times?

Possible answers to these questions reside, I think, in a moving letter from the parents of a six-year-old girl. The letter appeared, of all places, in *Parade* magazine. In addressing then President-elect Bush, the authors of the letter said that their daughter, "bright with excitement about the future," resembled and at the same time differed from children of an earlier time. "In her dreams of the future, she is 'a chemist, a choreographer, a hairdresser, a wife and mother,' " the parents wrote. "It is our job to help her get there. That's what our parents did for us and what their parents did for them. But it is no longer enough to love, feed, shelter, clothe, and educate a child," they warned in their state-of-the-union address, "not when the future itself is in danger. Being a conscientious parent today also means working to preserve and to protect the nation and the planet—now, before it's too late."

As these parents (Carl Sagan and Ann Druyan) suggest, there is much to be done (or redone) to protect our children not only from the threat of nuclear annihilation, but also from the Pentagon rhetoric justifying the proliferation of nuclear armaments. Such rhetoric, a kind of acid rain in the political atmosphere, seriously limits the possibilities for thoughtful debate on social issues in the United States and our ability to imagine alternative futures.

For forty years, in the name of peace, the country we love has justified ever-increasing expenditures for the development and deployment of evermore lethal weapons of war. These wartime priorities have been set and sustained by the executive, legislative, and judicial branches of government, without substantial opposition from the American public and with little reflection on the consequences, the dangers, and the costs involved.

Only recently have the economic consequences of nuclear stockpiling been publicly debated. The mass media began to address these central issues only after the decline of the American economy became obvious. In a recent cartoon in the Boston *Globe*, for example, a man reading a newspaper says to his neighbor: "If the Cold War is over, we'll need a monument." "We've got one," his friend replies, pointing to a badly dented old oil burner labeled "U.S. ECONOMY," rattling and wheezing, hissing and gasping in the background.

The failure of imagination in political and moral discourse is not surprising, however. As the novelist Gore Vidal has said: "Most Americans lack the words, the concepts that might help them figure out what has happened, ... and it is hardly their fault," he continued. "Simple falsities have been drummed into their heads from birth (socialism = Sweden = suicide), so that they will not rebel, not demand what is being withheld from them ... justice. Social justice."

For too long, loving one's country has been equated with being a kind of cheer leader for anything advocated in a White

House press release — government by public relations, one might call it. Such patriotism is reflected in chauvinist remarks about the United States being better than any other country (usually meaning richer and more powerful, militarily, than any other nation). Rarely is "better" associated with an openness to differing opinions and political controversy, to dissent and to freedom of inquiry. Repeatedly, in fact, public dissent, that right of citizenship, has been punished, with private citizens made subject to surveillance and harassment by agencies of the federal government.

In the fall of 1988, for example, the director of the F.B.I. talked to the U.S. Congress about the scope and duration of the bureau's investigation of political activists who opposed U.S. policy toward Nicaragua and El Salvador. The bureau had violated the attorney general's guidelines by placing an informant in one group and by collaborating with the army in El Salvador in its surveillance of U.S. and Salvadoran citizens. Other members of the Reagan administration, Oliver North and his associates, had actually been called "heroes" by the president when they equated patriotism with violation of the public trust.

LOVING ONE'S COUNTRY

Love of one's country is obviously a desirable trait to instill in our children; it is related to the value of loving oneself and one's culture and to recognizing the sacrifices and contributions of those who went before. But an uncritical acceptance of state authority leaves children unprepared for the responsibilities of citizenship and unwilling to address obvious injustices.

The essence of democracy, as the historian Paul Gagnon has said, is "open government and the public discussion of political problems, their solutions and the solutions' likely costs. . . . Murder is not the normal business of government proclaiming the rule of law." Besides, political dissent is often the principal way for minority opinion to become public, as was the case in protests against the Vietnam War, the draft, nuclear power, and nuclear weapons. Without the early protests at various nuclear installations and the public education surrounding them, we might never have heard about the disaster at Three Mile Island.

Such challenges to bureaucracy break down the walls of hope-lessness and indifference, freeing us to feel the urgency of issues in a nuclear age.

"Love of country precludes silence when an evil policy is being carried out by our own government," said Louise Ahrens, president of the Maryknoll Sisters, in congressional testimony criticizing U.S. policy in Central America. Love of country means supporting what is just as well as condemning what is unjust; it means committing oneself, at some level, to encour-aging humane values across a wide spectrum of social concerns.

Relearning patriotism also involves a new understanding of what leadership means and defining it as something more than the capacity to keep under cover the hard questions about U.S. behavior toward the rest of the world. Anyone thinking on this topic may feel as discouraged as Tom Ashbrook, in his reflec-tions about his native country after returning from ten years in Asia. Mr. Ashbrook posed the question "Where is our leader-ship?" He then brooded on the absence of leadership, as reflected in the presidential campaign of 1988: "Not political panderers or television shamans, but moral leaders of high sec-ular stripe, leaders of hardheaded vision who themselves project . . . honest courage. In America's blow-dried leadership waste-land, the rare standout . . . takes on an awkward sheen of saint-hood. Surely the ranks can be thickened, a broader banner raised."

The prospects for our enjoying such moral leadership are not encouraging, however, as the furor about "the flag" during the early months of the Bush administration indicated. The "polit-ical panderers" were out in force, denouncing the Supreme Court decision upholding the right of free speech (in this case, a citizen's burning the flag to protest U.S. foreign policy). Pres-ident Bush, appealing to the snallowest instincts of the chauvin-ist crowd, made a major issue of what, by any sober estimate, was a minor incident. What threat is posed to national honor, after all, what danger to public security, by that rare agitator who makes a spectacle of himself or herself by burning a flag? Should we all, like the stony-faced character in the *New Yorker* cartoon, sit on our porch with fire extinguisher and garden hose in hand, in anticipation of someone coming to torch the flag hanging from our front porch?

Instead of focusing on the central argument, that is, the protection of freedom of speech, which that flag stands for, Bush chose to make an icon of a piece of cloth, as if the symbol were the thing itself. Idolatry—blind adoration of something, a central theme in the Old Testament—is no more desirable in civil than it is in religious behavior. But in the wash of mindless, misplaced patriotism that followed the Supreme Court's decision, few men or women in leadership positions challenged the president's campaign for a constitutional amendment to ban desecration of the flag.

How might a responsible leader behave under such circumstances? And how might parents suggest to their children a more mature and responsible behavior than that represented by the president and many congressional leaders in this instance? If the stage has been set—that is, if children have come to expect a measured, mature response to controversy and conflict through discussion and mediation—then arguments over the proper response to protest, even to someone's burning the flag, will pose no major problem. Also, if their identity is linked not solely to nationhood, but to world citizenship, they are less likely to exalt "icons" and to confuse them with the essential concepts for which they stand.

We do well to treat the national flag—any national flag—with respect, as we might any piece of property that is important to us. And in making a statement about matters of public policy, one is wise not to offend others unnecessarily. In the history of the United States, nonetheless, there is a tradition of respecting people over property, and rebels and social critics have, on occasion, destroyed property in an effort to call attention to injustices tolerated by people in power.

Prior to the revolution against British rule, for example, citizens burned stamps and dumped tea in Boston Harbor. During the 1930s, farmers poured milk on the ground as a way of dramatizing the absence of fair prices for their labor. And in the late 1960s, Daniel Berrigan, Marjory Melville, Robert Cunnane, and James Forrest, among others, burned draft files, for conscience' sake, in an effort to give young men the option of *not* going to war in Southeast Asia.

Such incidents of civil disobedience are not so rare as textbooks in American history usually suggest; and the general principle they advance is central to moral teaching. Some explanation about the principle to children, when it comes up (along with reading a chapter or two of Howard Zinn's *People's History of the United States*, cited in the appendix), obviously serves the cause of citizenship. People *are* more important than property, and upholding that principle requires a thoughtful consideration of conflicting priorities—in deciding what can be and what cannot be allowed.

RESISTING ILLEGITIMATE AUTHORITY

Challenging or criticizing authority, while at the same time teaching children to respect authority, is a tricky business. For children the distinction between illegitimate and legitimate authority is, after all, almost impossible to make. In the early years, all adults are viewed as authority figures. Can one make distinctions, without at the same time hopelessly confusing children? In this situation, as in so many others in teaching values, the context varies, and discretion is essential.

As a teacher, for example, I tried to exercise extraordinary caution in criticizing our children's teachers. Even when their methods were ignorant, bordering on pernicious, I withheld judgment as long as I could, not because they deserved my support, but because my criticism might jeopardize their relationship—sound in other areas—with the children. In such matters, as in other areas of teaching values, a parent must recognize and respect children's limits, even while trusting their ability to make distinctions.

In retaining and conveying to one's children a respect for the good aspects of the national culture, a parent must at the same time encourage a critical attitude toward its history of injustice, discrimination, and chauvinism, particularly its behavior as an imperial power toward the poorer nations of the world. As with many nation-states, there is a dichotomy between American ideals and reality, between the hyperbole of Ronald Reagan's second inaugural address ("Peace is our highest aspiration, . . . we have never been aggressors") and the hard facts regarding numerous military interventions by the armed forces of the United States in foreign countries, not to mention its economic domination of them since World War II.

In a poem written during the period of the Vietnam War, Robert Bly characterized this split, bordering on schizophrenia, between reality and dream, between fact and hope, in these opening lines of "Those Being Eaten by America":

> I think of those being eaten by America
> Others, pale and soft, being stored
>   for later eating
> And Jefferson,
> who had hope in new oats.

Making room for these two sides of our history may encourage children to participate in the great debate about which history or tradition they wish to make their own.

Patriotism is a spiritual matter, the Reverend William Sloane Coffin argued in addressing the national conference of Pax Christi USA, "dealing, as it does, with choices and causes." My personal identity, for example, including my understanding of the meaning of life, is necessarily linked to my native land. The fact that one wing of the family has lived in New England since 1630 strongly influences my way of defining myself as a citizen; I see no need, for that reason, to prove to anyone that *I* am an American. Another wing of the family homesteaded in the Midwest and the Southwest, so I have powerful links to those regions, where "the wide open spaces" helped to define my social attitude, a kind of missionary mentality, perhaps, associated with exploration and struggle.

For the present generation, growing up during the time of the Reagan and Bush administrations, "patriotism" may be defined in a very narrow way, as unquestioned loyalty toward whatever they are told by authority figures. Certainly since World War II, the trappings of empire have been everywhere more evident in public assemblies in the United States: the presence of the American flag in church sanctuaries, for example;

opening most public events, including concerts, with singing "The Star Spangled Banner," or pledging allegiance to the flag. State architecture, particularly in the courts, has become increasingly imperial. I was struck by this fact recently in attending a trial in the U.S. District Court, Hartford, Connecticut, where the judge's bench and background resembled an altar, with an enormous backdrop in gold framed by an arch with large gold stars. What ordinary citizen could retain his or her composure before such trappings? What place had all this awe-inspiring regalia and paraphernalia in a people's court?

Such settings and rituals are characteristic, nonetheless, of public life in the United States, as are continual interventions in the Third World and popular films extolling our triumphs elsewhere; in this context, our children, like ourselves, begin to define themselves as citizens.

In other words, one must not dismiss as irrelevant either a child's — or a grownup's — feelings of and attitude toward patriotism; nor should one intentionally offend those feelings, for they have profound cultural and religious implications. One way of respecting these feelings, while questioning the manner of expressing them, is to offer a positive alternative, such as shifting our allegiance from the symbols of the nationalistic state to the symbols of the land itself: from the flag, for example, to photographs and graphics of the magnificent landscape. "Far more than the flag, the land itself is the primal symbol of America and now is the time," as Sam Smith has said, "when we need to save that land from rampant destruction."

Another way of respecting patriotism is to encourage, in our own children, a kind of "lover's quarrel" with their country, appreciating the strengths and correcting the weaknesses. For the best patriots, as William Sloane Coffin has argued, "are not uncritical lovers of their country any more than they are loveless critics of it." True patriots carry on a "lover's quarrel with their country, a reflection, as we understand it, of God's eternal quarrel with the world."

In contemporary America, that lover's quarrel will necessarily involve taking a critical stance toward our situation if we are to recover several alternative traditions from the past. In doing so, we may want to follow the example of men and women who had little regard for the "macho," "imperial" attitudes espoused by recent presidents and public figures. We will value public figures such as Senator Mark O. Hatfield of Oregon, who voted repeatedly, as "a majority of one," against nerve gas production, underground testing, MX missiles, the draft, and SDI; "peace through strength is a fallacy," he argued during a vote on military appropriations in August 1989, "for peace is not simply the absence of a nuclear holocaust." And we will try to reclaim a broader, more humane, and less nationalistic definition of citizenship, associated with figures such as Thomas Paine, Henry David Thoreau, Lucy Stone, Eugene Victor Debs, Jane Addams, Dorothy Day, and Martin Luther King—each of them American to the core, but ultimately, as well, citizens of the world.

7

Claiming a Tradition

Our country is the world; our countrymen are all mankind.
— William Lloyd Garrison
"Declaration of Sentiments, 1838"

And if [our children] are not active participating citizens —
small-d democrats — it may be because we aren't.
— Ellen Goodman
"When the Moral Life of Children
Jabs at Adults"

Thus far, I have pointed to some historical facts and social conditions that complicate our efforts to be authentic parents and citizens. I have suggested also, in passing, specific courses of action and "what is to be done." In learning to become "citizens of the world" and in helping our children understand that concept, we have a number of examples, models, and resources available to us, some from the past, some from recent history. This chapter describes four traditions, indigenous to American culture, that might inform and support parents in their efforts to teach social values to children.

Every period of American history, from precolonial times to the present, and every region of this country have harbored men and women attentive to and courageous enough to resist the injustices and stupidities of their time.

William Lloyd Garrison, the great nineteenth-century abolitionist whose motto appears beneath this chapter's heading and whose writings suggested the theme of this book, is a member of that group. With a host of other Americans, he offers, in his life and values, an alternative to the competition and aggression that have dominated private and public lives in this country in recent decades. In working to abolish capital punishment and slavery, Garrison represented a tradition of personal courage and public responsibility in which children might take an interest, if they are lucky enough to hear about it from their parents or elders.

Born in Newburyport, Massachusetts, in 1805, William Lloyd Garrison grew up in a strict evangelical household. As a young man, his commitment to ending slavery was set aflame by his being arrested in Baltimore after attempting to halt slaveships leaving that port. Following his release, he returned to Boston to work as an editor and agitator for the immediate and complete abolition of slavery. Undergirding his efforts was a lifelong dedication to social justice, which included an insistence, against considerable opposition, that women occupy key positions in antislavery societies. He once broke up a meeting of one antislavery society and formed another, in fact, in protest against women being denied places of authority and leadership in the international crusade against slavery.

As with most people, Garrison was no "saint," and his life was not without its contradictions: an apostle of nonviolence, he nonetheless justified the Civil War as a kind of holy war. Prior to that, he was, nonetheless, a beacon to others who were militant against slavery: Frederick Douglass, the black abolitionist and editor; Abigail Kelley Foster, feminist and editor of *The Anti-Slavery Bugle*; Adin Ballou, founder of the Hopedale Community, with whom Garrison cofounded the New England Non-Resistance Society in 1838; William Greenleaf Whittier, the Quaker poet; and countless other citizens. Although Garrison's motto (quoted above, from the masthead of *The Liberator)* sounds sexist to our newly tuned ears, his emphasis upon world citizenship *is* surprisingly modern, focusing attention on a person's responsibility as a citizen in a global village.

Frederick Douglass escaped from slavery, journeyed to Boston, and apprenticed himself to Garrison before going off to found a newspaper and to build another antislavery following, in Rochester, New York. Similarly, Abigail Kelley Foster, "who cleared a path across which many women walked to freedom," was one of Garrison's ardent disciples; as a young woman, she gave up teaching in order to devote her life to freeing the slaves. Through her, many others, such as Lucy Stone — the first woman to speak from a pulpit in Massachusetts — took up the cause of women. Through communities of this kind, a culture that had tolerated injustice toward blacks and women began to transform itself, much as we are required to transform the practices and institutions of our own time (many of them a direct result of concentrations of wealth and inadequate responses to "the cries of the poor").

Garrison's internationalist sentiments reflected, of course, a still earlier patriot, Thomas Paine, whose motto was "My country is the world; to do good is my religion." Martin Luther King, in a famous speech condemning U.S. policy in Vietnam, returned to this theme: "I speak as a citizen of the world," he said in 1967, "for the world as it stands aghast at the path we have taken." Through these remarkable figures of the eighteenth, nineteenth, and twentieth centuries, and countless others, there is a tradition of citizenship based upon noble values, one that waits to be reclaimed by "ordinary people" of this country.

How, then, does a parent make this tradition of social justice accessible to children? Not by lecturing them about it, certainly; and not by waiting for them to learn about it in school, since many school systems — and even colleges — succeed remarkably well in keeping this tradition out of the curriculum. Much of children's formal education, in fact, leads them to think that the only way to "succeed" is to ape the dominant culture of competition and greed, violence and conformity.

In this, as in so many aspects of teaching values, a parent brings an alternative tradition to life by making it visible in the home. A father presents heroes and heroines as "family," as flawed and resourceful people-in-struggle, rather than as "larger than life" and, therefore, as people inaccessible to children.

Although one would hardly know it from the values that presently characterize the behavior of many individuals and public institutions, several dormant American traditions embody values that might sustain our children as well as ourselves in the years ahead. Parents have a responsibility to claim those traditions, to make them visible and accessible to our children. We can do that by the way we live, through the people, communities, and cultural traditions we identify with—particularly the following four traditions from the American experience.

A TRADITION OF NONVIOLENCE

From the eighteenth century (or even earlier) until the present—in the movement for independence, through the abolitionist, feminist, labor, and antiwar movements—a tradition of nonviolence has informed the history of the United States. In each case, citizens brought about substantial social change, resisting oppression and alleviating injustice, without resorting to war and violence. Much of the movement for independence was accomplished, according to John Adams, in the "hearts and minds of the people," long before the colonists took up arms against the British.

Similarly, nonviolent resistance to slavery, particularly in the northern states, succeeded in a way that violence could not in the Civil War. Working people won decent wages and working conditions through peaceful protest, including sit-down strikes and well-orchestrated publicity efforts and public education, as in the United Auto Workers strike in Flint, Michigan, in 1935. Throughout these campaigns, various apostles of nonviolence sought not defeat of the antagonist, but reconciliation, as Martin Luther King said in "Loving Your Enemies" (1957).

Central to the history of nonviolence in the United States are the lives and writings of John Woolman, Garrison, Adin Ballou, Eugene Victor Debs, and, more recently, King, Dorothy Day, Paul Goodman, Mulford Sibley, Thomas Merton, Barbara Deming, David Dellinger, and Daniel and Philip Berrigan.

In various struggles on behalf of women's rights, civil rights, and nuclear disarmament, a significant community of people have persistently counseled against violence in fighting injustice. Henry David Thoreau and his contemporary, Bronson Alcott, went to jail rather than pay taxes to support a war that would "shed innocent blood." During the First and Second World Wars and the Korean and Vietnam Wars, thousands of young men went to jail rather than take up arms against their brothers and sisters. Since 1980, in symbolic actions on the side of life, the Plowshares communities have disarmed nuclear weapons and nuclear submarines in Pennsylvania, Florida, Minnesota, Rhode Island, Missouri, Michigan, Texas, Wisconsin, Colorado, California, Massachusetts, Virginia, Connecticut, as well as West Germany and Australia.

The fact that these actions often received little attention in the mass media, even as the participants risked and sometimes endured harsh sentences for conscience' sake, dramatizes the need for people to rely on alternative publications for news about nonviolent movements for social change in our time.

A TRADITION OF DISSENT

Slogans associated with the tradition of dissent against illegitimate authority in American history include the following: "Don't tread on me." "No taxation without representation." "Don't mourn, organize." "We shall overcome." To these may be added a saying that echoes the theme of this book: "Think globally, act locally," as well as the motto, based upon the writings of the prophet Isaiah, of dissenters now in prison for speaking out against the imminent peril posed by nuclear weapons: "Beat swords into plowshares and spears into pruning hooks."

The tradition of dissent has its roots in the early British settlements on this continent, when Quakers and others spoke out against laws circumscribing their religious freedom. Some four hundred pamphlets that espoused dissenting ideas regarding British rule were published in the American colonies long before Thomas Paine echoed them in *Common Sense* or Thomas Jefferson gave them eloquent voice in the Declaration of Independence. Since then, every effort to correct injustice has owed much to dissenters who willingly risked harassment and imprisonment in resisting unjust laws. Also, years before Congress passed legislation for American women to vote, or for southern blacks to enjoy protection under the law, respectively, Abigail Kelley Foster refused to pay taxes in Massachusetts and Rosa

Parks refused to obey a discriminatory law in Alabama, in their efforts to build a just society.

Writings central to the tradition of dissent include, in addition to the Declaration of Independence, Henry David Thoreau's "Civil Disobedience," the speeches of Eugene Victor Debs and Emma Goldman, the essays of Randolph Bourne and, more recently, of Howard Zinn and Noam Chomsky, and Martin Luther King's "Letter from Birmingham Jail." American journalism owes much to editors such as Isaiah Thomas and Garrison, whose publications strengthened freedom of the press in the early years of the country, as well as to people such as Daniel Ellsberg, who risked harassment and imprisonment in order to tell disturbing truths about government secrecy and duplicity regarding the war in Southeast Asia.

Songs and ballads related to this tradition include those of Joe Hill, an early twentieth-century hero of the labor movement. Workers advocating better working conditions and better pay, frequently arrested for speaking on the street, decided to follow the example of the Salvation Army and to sing their message instead. Writing new words to old gospel hymns, Hill, "the Wobblie balladeer," inspired a host of folk singers who supported and contributed to the tradition of dissent in the 1930s, 1960s, and on to the present: Woody Guthrie, Pete Seeger, Utah Phillips, Joan Baez, Phil Ochs, Holly Near, and Charlie King. Children, particularly, are often charmed by their songs and ballads, from "This Land Is Your Land" and "Roll On, Columbia," to "What Did You Learn in School Today?," "I Dreamed I Saw Joe Hill, Last Night," and Holly Near's "Foolish Notion," with its plaintive refrain: "Why do we kill people who are killing people / To show that killing people is wrong?"

A TRADITION OF PEACE CHURCHES

A unique characteristic of the so-called radical tradition in the United States, with links to our anti-imperial and anticolonial birthright, is its strong religious association, particularly to historic peace churches—the Quakers, Mennonites, and Church of the Brethren. Through their witness, including utopian communities, congregations, schools and colleges, and alternative presses and publishing houses, they protected the right of freedom of conscience and kept alive a vision of a world without war. Over several decades, they established an alternative, within the Selective Service System, for those who, in conscience, objected to participation in war or who wanted no part of the military effort. Since the 1960s, a larger audience has learned what these churches have to teach—how to maintain values relating to peace and social justice and how to teach them to children.

Through various religious publications, such as *Friends Journal* and *Conciliation Quarterly Newsletter* (a Mennonite publication) the historic peace churches offer valuable resources for families, churches, schools, and the wider community. The Friends Committee on National Legislation (245 Second Street, N.E., Washington, DC 20002) provides up-to-date information on pending legislation in Congress on issues of social justice, as do regional offices of American Friends Service Committee throughout the U.S.

For centuries, the peace churches have been a powerful influence, far beyond their actual numbers, in upholding the dignity of all human persons. Quakers were among the first abolitionists, and all three churches, through the experience of their members, have much to teach about espousing and living values in conflict with the dominant culture. For them, nonviolence is not merely a method of initiating change, but a way of life. Organizations that remained steadfast in their commitment to peace originated from these churches, including several associations that sprang up around the time of World War I: Women's International League for Peace and Freedom, American Friends Service Committee, Fellowship of Reconciliation, War Resisters League, and, later, the Central Committee for Conscientious Objectors.

In recent years, the religious witness for social justice has moved beyond the historic peace churches to the larger denominations. The Roman Catholic bishops, the Presbyterian and Methodist churches, among others, have published statements on conscientious objection and nuclear disarmament, and in some areas of the country the institutional church strongly supports illegal aliens who fled repressive military regimes in Latin America. Recent pastoral letters on the arms race and economic justice reflect the experience of religious and lay men and women working among the poor in this country and abroad.

A TRADITION OF ENVIRONMENTAL CONCERN

The first inhabitants of this continent, the Native Americans, who were victimized by exploitative values now threatening the survival of our planet, advocated our being "good neighbors of the earth." Over the past two centuries, a substantial and vocal minority has joined them, including poets, essayists, naturalists, and social critics such as Henry David Thoreau, John Muir, John Burroughs, Rachel Carson, Helen and Scott Nearing, and Wendell Berry. The Sierra Club, Friends of the Earth, the Audubon Society, Greenpeace, and similar organizations are part of a tradition encouraging careful study and protection of ecological resources: wetlands, woodlands, wild shores, and rivers.

The construction of uranium foundries and processing plants for nuclear power and weapons, beginning in the 1950s, seriously threatens the delicate balance of nature. At times, a careless and sometimes dishonest Atomic Energy Commission assured people that such operations created, as one of its communiques said, "no environmental, toxic or radiological hazards." John Glenn, senator from Ohio, writing in the *New York Times*, has argued that these communiques were the first in a "long line of deceptions and betrayals of the public trust," and were followed by many episodes in which the government "violated its own worker health and safety standards," even ordering private contractors to ignore state and federal environmental laws.

Gradually, ordinary citizens began to recognize the harmful effects of this "environmental time bomb," as Senator Glenn called it. The ecological damage to the environment by nuclear power and weapons plants and by nuclear waste includes a high incidence of cancer among people and animals near nuclear testing sites in Nevada, Utah, New Mexico, and elsewhere in the country. Had it not been for the effort of the courageous people, members of the Clamshell Alliance, who risked arrest and imprisonment in Seabrook, New Hampshire, for example, we might never have gotten a full disclosure about Three Mile Island, which contaminated large residential and work areas in

Pennsylvania. Since official policymakers are often reactive rather than active in concerning themselves with the public's welfare, ordinary citizens must remain attentive to the intimate connection between themselves and the environment, and insist upon policies that recognize that interdependence.

Encouraging people to become friends of the earth and of people indigenous to every region, the movement reached the general public only in recent years; it exposed the harmful effects of pollution—from oil spills, waste dumps, and industrial garbage—on the water supply, fish, and other oceanic life. Gradually, ordinary citizens have begun to recognize the close connections between people's issues and environmental issues in the struggle for social justice.

●

Frequently, of course, these four traditions—nonviolence, dissent, the peace churches, and ecology—overlap. Each has offered and continues to offer a variety of approaches and perspectives, depending upon the times and the issues. Abigail Kelley Foster, for example, the great abolitionist, born into an Irish Quaker family in 1811, also inspired many who championed the rights of women. Walt Whitman, who lost his position as editor of a Brooklyn newspaper because of his militant abolitionism, carried the tradition of dissent in his blood. From his father, who had known Thomas Paine, he learned about the author of *Common Sense* and made Paine's values central to his poetry. Both Paine and Whitman had been born into families associated with the Society of Friends. And Whitman, in turn, inspired John Burroughs, who was also a friend of John Muir, essayist, passionate conservationist, and founder of The Sierra Club. Several recent poets, Denise Levertov, Stanley Kunitz, and Robert Bly, and folk singers Woody Guthrie and Pete Seeger have not only written about but also actively supported campaigns against nuclear weapons and on behalf of environmental protection.

Crucially important to today's parents and children, all four of these traditions live on in the choices and the inspiration offered by individuals—men and women of every race and economic background—families, communities, and organizations.

Accounts of alternative ways of living, in keeping with these traditions, are accessible not only in biographies and histories, but also from people and publications in every area of the United States at this very moment. We need them to remind us of the importance of creative dissent and, at times, nonviolent civil disobedience against unjust laws; they need us, in return, for support and encouragement. In the appendix, I mention a few representative children's books about people and social movements loyal to each of the four traditions, as well as contemporary organizations and agencies that "carry them on."

HOMETOWN HEROES AND HEROINES: LOCAL HISTORY

Parents can keep themselves and their families in close touch with liberation struggles today and in earlier times by centering their attention on local history and the experience of local citizens involved in these efforts. Too often, children grow up thinking that history always happened somewhere else, not in their own town or region. Yet almost any major movement among workers, minorities, and women involved people across the United States, and nationally known figures came to prominence, first, through agitation and organizing in their own town or region.

Thomas Paine, for example, gained his first experience in political rabble rousing in his native England, lobbying for higher wages for excisemen, before coming to the colonies and writing *Common Sense* and *The American Crisis*. Similarly, Eugene Victor Debs achieved local fame in Terre Haute, Indiana, as a member of the railroad workers' union there, before moving on to Illinois and the famous Pullman Strike that radicalized him and made him a socialist. Pushed by Peter Maurin to start a newspaper, Dorothy Day first distributed the *Catholic Worker* at Union Square, near her native Brooklyn; this was much before she and her associates carried the movement to cities and farms in New England, the Midwest, the South, and the Far West, and eventually to Europe and Australia. How many young people, growing up in Terre Haute or Brooklyn, learn about the remarkable heroes and heroines native to their ground?

Growing up in Oklahoma, for example, I heard little in school about the rich populist tradition that characterized the state from its very beginnings. Though I benefited from those values, in the priorities the early settlers gave to public education, I knew nothing about the people responsible for establishing them — early settlers, admirers of Eugene Victor Debs and other native American socialists, who helped to build a strong democratic consensus among the people. Only accidentally, through a student folk singer at the university in the 1950s, did I first hear the songs of Woody Guthrie — some of the great cultural artifacts of the region, permeated as they are by values of social justice. Guthrie's "This Land Is Your Land," as someone has said, ought to be our national anthem: in addition to espousing democratic values and working-class sympathies, it's a song that everyone can sing.

Later, I moved to another region of the country, the Northeast, famous for its place in the early history of the United States, only to discover that people growing up in my new home town knew almost nothing about the rich literary and social history that was theirs: the facts that their city, Worcester, Massachusetts, had sent local citizens to homestead in the new state of Kansas, to assure its entering the union on the side of abolitionism, and had hosted one of the first national conventions of women, were unknown to them. Similarly, in the twentieth century, the area had harbored several leading labor agitators, poets, and social critics. Thus do we grow up impoverished because of our loss of memory about the people, occasions, and events that contributed to our enjoying certain "inalienable" rights of citizenship.

FORMAL STUDY

Parents may also wish to make available to themselves and their children the opportunities offered by academic courses and programs now known as peace studies, which are common in colleges and universities and sometimes in public schools. As an academic discipline, peace studies had its origin in the International Peace Research Association and the Consortium on Peace Research, Education, and Development, both indebted

to the economist Kenneth Boulding and to the sociologist Elise
Boulding, husband and wife, parents and grandparents.

Peace studies or peace and world security studies — understood here as "the systematic interdisciplinary study of the
causes of war and the conditions of peace" — came into being
because some teachers, scholars, and researchers wished to
remember and to make room in the classroom for the many
invisible victims of war and oppression throughout the world. In
teaching history, physics, psychology, government, or literature
classes, they argued that victims of violence and neglect — often
invisible and voiceless, as far as the industrial nations are concerned — have a special claim on our attention.

Since the late 1960s, academics in disciplines as various as
physics, religion, anthropology, and biology have been vocal
about the university's failure to address the broader implications
of foreign and domestic policies, in this country and abroad: the
danger posed to the planet, its people, species of plants, animals,
birds, and fishes by the nuclear arms race, the pollution of rivers
and underground water sources, and the destruction of rain forests. And throughout the world, thousands of nongovernmental
agencies — citizen groups practicing citizen diplomacy — have
organized themselves to protect people and natural resources
threatened by policymakers and corporate bodies, both public
and private, who destroy or exploit the resources of the earth.
The size and number of such nongovernmental agencies are
impressive. A few of these are: the Union of Concerned Scientists, Physicians for Social Responsibility, Neighbor to Neighbor, Beyond War, and Greenpeace (or the Campaign for
Nuclear Disarmament and the Greenham Common Women in
England). Their actions range from interfering with the launching of a $1.2 billion trident submarine at New London, Connecticut, in 1989, to firsthand research into the conditions of
refugee groups, famine, and human rights' abuses in Africa,
Mexico, and Southeast Asia.

As is often the case, educational institutions, particularly universities, have been slow in responding to this movement, but
in 1964, a group of international scholars initiated the International Peace Research Association, using their academic skills
to study the efforts to enhance and to build peace and security

systems. Some teachers and scholars began to say: "We offer courses on the Literature of the First World War, the History of the Civil War, the Psychology of Aggression, and so on, but very few courses on, for example, the Theology of Peace, the Psychological Effects of Nuclear War on Children, or the Theory and Practice of Nonviolence from Tolstoi and Gandhi, to Dorothy Day and Martin Luther King."

Shortly thereafter, physicians, biologists, and social scientists founded research centers related to peace studies at Harvard, Yale, and the University of Colorado. In the early 1980s, faculty from various academic backgrounds began offering an interdisciplinary course called Perspectives on Nuclear War at the University of Wisconsin, Madison, initiated and coordinated by a professor of literature. Similar programs now thrive at Notre Dame, Tufts, Syracuse, and many other universities.

The shadow side of this movement's history is the organized opposition that some peace studies programs face from old Cold Warriors on campuses across the country. Not surprisingly, those academics who have dominated and controlled "war" policy studies since World War II take a dim view of peace studies. Some academics have even accused peace studies of having an ideological bias — on the grounds, usually, that professors who endorse U.S. policy are objective and scholarly, while those who question U.S. policy are subjective and unacademic. Much of that criticism can be dismissed as being based on "pork barrel" politics, reminding us that teachers and researchers hustling Pentagon dollars are no more attractive or intellectual in their deportment than politicians or defense contractors engaged in similar scams.

Dependent upon the ecosphere, we are an endangered species. And without significant changes in priorities, as the Union of Concerned Scientists and others have warned us, we may be broiled or steamed by the poisonous gases from our automobiles even before we are fricasseed by a nuclear or neutron bomb. As parents, we need to develop means, related to our competence, to resist people and systems that threaten global health and security and to explore alternative ways of being in the world and assuring a human future.

Peace studies extends this effort into the classroom, making it part of our children's formal education. Until we develop sophisticated, philosophically based, structured, and well-researched techniques and skills for teaching peace, as the biologist Mary E. Clark has said, "we shall never succeed in outgrowing our moral adolescence." Those skills include methods of resolving conflict, with awareness as well as understanding of how our own values impede "our ability to empathize with those holding different visions."

Through engaged learning and active participation, as citizens and teachers of values, we manage to "hear" voices, occasionally, that belong to victims of war and oppression—past, present, and potential victims. Traditionally, university students—most visibly during the 1960s—have raised their voices in opposition to people and structures responsible for victimizing people in Vietnam, then South Africa, Central America, and the homeless millions in the United States. So it is encouraging that teachers and scholars in various disciplines are beginning to design courses and to pursue research that center on a commitment to "positive peace," rather than on sentiments about being "anti-war."

In a remarkable essay entitled "Poet and State," in his collected essays, Stanley Kunitz wrote, "[Humanity] will perish unless [we] learn that the web of the universe is a continuous tissue. Touch it at any point, and the whole web shudders." Unknowingly perhaps, Kunitz used a metaphor describing the tenuousness of the earth that Chief Seattle used, in 1854, at the time his ancestral Indian lands were transferred to the federal government: "Whatever befalls the earth befalls the sons of the earth. Man did not weave the web of life; he is merely a strand in it. Whatever he does to the web, he does to himself."

Peace studies is a new academic effort to protect and strengthen that tenuous, beautiful web. Parents engaged in teaching values to their children will perhaps see their effort as related to it; they may find help and encouragement, as well, in the tradition of nonviolence and dissent, and in the experience of those associated with it. Thus do we claim a tradition to support our effort to build communities of responsible people.

8

BUILDING COMMUNITY

When solitaries draw close, releasing
each solitude into its blossoming, . . .

Great power flows from us
luminous, a promise. Yes!
— Denise Levertov
    "Political Action in Which Each Individual
    Acts from the Heart"

Being part of a community fulfills something central to our
understanding of ourselves as human beings, as social beings
dependent upon and responsible for others. Children thrive in
the midst of supportive communities, where they feel wanted
and their futures seem secure. In their autobiographies, writers,
artists, and public figures, particularly those who retain a strong
sense of themselves, often emphasize the importance of
extended family and a community of friends during their early
years. People as diverse as Katherine Anne Porter, Dorothy
Day, Eudora Welty, Maya Angelou, and Reynolds Price have
described in detail their sense, early on, of being members of a
lively, value-laden community.

In fiction and poetry, as well as in religious writings, people
frequently "find" themselves as they become more aware of their
connectedness to others. In "The River," a short story by Flannery O'Connor, for example, Bevel, a young boy, discovers his

105

lost sense of belonging after meeting a backwoods preacher. Unlike Bevel's parents, who treat everything he says or does as a joke, the preacher takes the boy seriously. Baptizing Bevel during a revival at the river, the preacher swings the boy "upside down and plunged his head into the water . . . then jerked him up again and looked sternly at the gasping child. . . . 'You count now,' the preacher said. 'You didn't even count before.' "

In *I Know Why the Caged Bird Sings*, Maya Angelou describes a similar initiation into a moral universe, in a tale about her grandmother's humiliation before and eventual moral triumph over "powhite trash."

We build community through a long, concrete, and subtle process of helping one another realize that we "count," one by one. Through rituals, parents convey to children that they are important — to family and community — and help children appreciate their place in the great drama of human history. The sacraments and rites of passage in the world's religions, such as baptism and confirmation, if they are properly prepared for and carried out, serve that purpose. Through such communal experiences, children grow up being aware of a "culture" that informs and sustains them.

Pictures of themselves and their parents, grandparents, other relatives, and friends are obvious signs, to children, that they have a history; but as they grow older books, paintings, films, and visits to historical sites make them conscious of a community beyond the family. Growing into adulthood, even as they decide to rebel against inherited values, they at least know where they are *frum*, as Flannery O'Connor put it. For such children, history is not a void; it is a presence to be accepted or rejected in the life-long process of development, of individuation and socialization.

As a teacher, I am struck again and again by how family values, including those relating to social justice, get passed along from grandparents, aunts and uncles, and parents to young people. Last spring, at a student display for the annual peace fair in our city, parents of two student-organizers joined their college-age children in blowing up earth balloons and passing out leaflets to the crowd, telling about the theory and practice of nonviolence. It is hardly surprising, therefore, that these parents' sons regularly commit themselves to raising money for Oxfam, sponsoring programs on Nicaragua and South Africa, or preparing a monthly meal for homeless people at a local Catholic Worker House. And when they decided to commit civil disobedience at Seabrook, to protest the opening of a hazardous nuclear power plant, they did so, as they indicated by a report to their classmates, out of an awareness of their connections to their younger brothers and sisters, and the next generation.

Children "whose family love energizes a communal inclination," as Dr. Robert Coles has suggested, "share a political cause (eros)." And Denise Levertov's "Political Action in Which Each Individual Acts from the Heart"—quoted at the beginning of this chapter—evokes that same communal feeling, when children learn to give themselves to cooperative efforts for the welfare of others.

The family, the first means of socialization, is the rightful place to learn, to nurture, and to encourage children to see the links between themselves and the community or, as it is understood by psychologists, between the demands of the ego and the responsibilities of citizenship. Political philosophers and social psychologists, from Plato and Aristotle to Hobbes, Locke, Rousseau, and Engles, have been preoccupied with that relationship for centuries. More recently, Dr. Coles has documented the fact that children's imaginations "are charged by continuing participation in family politics" and a tendency to associate the workings of the family and the larger world.

Children of authoritarian fathers and dominating mothers, on the other hand, have difficulty imagining themselves as participants in governance or as "actors" in a democratic society. Similarly, people who had a weak sense of their belonging to anyone when they were young may carry that sense of alienation into adolescence and adulthood.

I often sense the limited awareness of community among young college students, particularly within the last decade or so. Talented and conscientious, they seldom feel much responsibility for others beyond a small circle of friends. Not surprisingly, they are also rather fragile, sometimes demoralized and confused by the harsh realities that await them: large indebtedness because of their college loans, a limited job market, and considerable uncertainty about marriage and raising a family. In recent years, students have brought uncommon problems to my attention, ranging from the effects of family divorces and deaths from AIDS or cancer, to heroic efforts on their parts to help friends recover from alcohol or drug dependency—involvements and responsibilities that were simply unknown, on such a large scale, to students of my generation.

At the same time, adolescents, from junior high school through college, are increasingly subject to deep depressions, as the suicide rate among them suggests. Significant changes in our culture make it necessary for adults to develop new skills in preventing and repairing the psychological damage done to our children, and further disintegration of community. "Our understandable wish to preserve the planet," as the poet Wendell Berry has said, "must somehow be reduced to the scale of our competence—that is, the wish to preserve all of its humble households and neighborhoods." In doing so, where do parents look for help?

From the time of the Puritans, our society has recognized the importance of community and of individuals acting for the common good, especially through the experimental communities of the nineteenth and twentieth centuries—Brook Farm, Fruitlands, Hopedale, Oneida, the Catholic Worker. "They gave the American experiment as a whole a utopian touch that it has never lost, in spite of all our failings," as Robert N. Bellah has said in his study of individualism and commitment in American life. Through an awareness of this history and of various means at their disposal, parents can encourage and strengthen that communal spirit among their children.

FAMILY MEETINGS

Learning empathy for others and our dependence upon them—in the family as well as in the global village—is accomplished in part by children having a sense of their own worth and integrity. They learn to depend on others when they know they "count" in the family unit, as well as in the eyes of their parents. One way to affirm a child's self-worth is to give him or her a voice in family decisions whenever possible, particularly regarding those matters that affect each person in the family: decisions about sharing the work load—cooking, house cleaning, laundry, weekly chores—as well as about sharing financial resources, space, the family automobile, and the future.

One useful mechanism for such discussions and decisions is the weekly (or at least periodic) family meeting, where each person has a chance to speak—where, in fact, each person *must* speak, if only to voice his or her thoughts and feelings about matters of interest to the group.

I mention this approach admitting immediately that my family seldom used it as effectively or as often as we might have. Our family meetings were at first chaotic, usually improvised during suppertime, several of us talking at once and my guts grinding as I fried hamburgers and passed the potato chips and kept the milk carton circulating, and my wife refereed discussions from the other end of the table. Eventually, however, when we called a meeting, insisting that each person speak so that the older, more articulate children didn't always dominate the discussion, it helped to mediate disputes and to dissipate hurt feelings. Such meetings also dramatized the fact that someone who was not necessarily the loudest and fastest talker might make sense and that even the youngest child had important contributions to make.

Having a sense of community, like charity, begins at home. A parent's task is to encourage children's awareness and to strengthen, little by little, their self-confidence, first in the family, then in the neighborhood, then at school. Thus do young people learn to become active rather than passive citizens.

As long as children feel safe to express their fears, anxieties, and deepest loves at home, venturing into the wider world will not threaten them, although doing so is a delicate process, nonetheless. School, the first major move outside the home, may be a relatively simple transition if it's a neighborhood school. Moving from there into middle or junior high school, however, may evoke stronger reactions, in part because of the physical and psychological changes flooding in, and the more complicated social problems children confront for the first time.

For four of our six children, the first days and weeks of junior high school, for example, were traumatic, provoking nightmares, fears of other students stealing their books and tormenting them, and a wholesale dread of the large classrooms. (Now one of those children teaches in the junior high school he attended, and the environment is even more threatening than it was ten years ago: larger classes, fewer teachers, drugs, teenage pregnancy, a larger percentage of children from broken homes.) The task of helping children to negotiate their way through a complicated meritocracy is more demanding than ever. In this effort, parents can rely on some traditional means and some new approaches, as they assist their progeny in making the transition from childhood to adulthood.

CELEBRATIONS

If the family is the context in which children learn the value of community, it is also the context in which to celebrate it, through events and rituals that call attention to what people have accomplished for the welfare of others. Parents need to give some thought to the manner in which they observe holidays, in order to remind children of the social values which they cherish and to inform them about their own history. Our celebrating birthdays, anniversaries, and liturgies commemorating people to whom we are grateful reminds us of their courageous deeds and writings; it gives our children access to a wider community and to the places, books, and artifacts associated with it.

Years ago, one of our closest friends—father to a brood—insisted upon our reading the Declaration of Independence during our Fourth of July picnic, each child and adult taking a phrase or paragraph. So in the midst of the heat, wet diapers, burnt hamburgers, and (inevitably) at least one bleeding foot, Jefferson's noble document did get a hearing. Now, two decades later, with members of both families scattered over the Western hemisphere, we still read the Declaration of Independence, recapturing for a few moments that eighteenth-century spirit, when people of this country believed government was for the living. It's still a stirring document, a concrete and economical summary of the intellectual origins of American democractic ideals.

Any family activity of this kind, of course, must combine celebration and education as unobtrusively as possible. For the newest major holiday, January 15 — a glum, wintry day in our region — a paragraph or two from one of Martin Luther King's speeches brighten any commemorative prayer or celebration. This reading emphasizes, all the while, the interdependence of all people and the central place of love in nonviolent social change, as King said in "Letter from Birmingham Jail."

How one defines one's community determines, at times, one's stance before the rest of the world: who is included, who excluded. Narrow definitions of that community can make people insular, hostile to others of a different race or sex or religion. Immersed in the values of a narrowly defined group, people sometimes create their own ghettos or asylums, with the "inmates" thinking of themselves as beings apart from the rest of humanity.

Encouraging children's sense of belonging to a global family means taking advantage of opportunities to acquaint them with people from other cultures. Increasingly, through cooperative programs in this country and abroad, in schools and colleges, as well as internships with groups involved in "people-to-people diplomacy," young people learn how it feels to walk for awhile in the moccasins of another person, as the Native American saying has it. "There must be not only a vision of the global family, but also a sufficient sense of belonging to that global family," as Robert McAfee Brown has said, "so that people will undertake risks on behalf of it."

Among several excellent books indicating how we resemble and differ from other people — and why everyone deserves respect and tolerance — I am particularly fond of *People*, written and illustrated by Peter Spier. Large and handsome, with drawings of eyes, shapes, noses, clothes, games, homes, feasts, pets, foods, and artifacts, and with scripts for many of the world's languages, it is a good book for parents to read with very young children, from age three on up. The following saying, from the Greek poet Menander, quoted on the title page, suggests the value of knowing other cultures: "In many ways the saying 'know thyself' is not well said. It were more practical to say 'know other people!' "

HOMEMADE ACTIVITIES FOR BUILDING COMMUNITY

Initiating children into democratic practices, and helping them to feel at ease therein, best begins in the family. These practices can be made visible in numerous ways, subtle as well as direct. Here are a few approaches:

1. Set aside a bulletin board or other space in the house for leaflets, cartoons, bumper stickers, and articles that address important social issues. Children, including teenagers rebelling against their parents—who automatically disregard anything you *say* to them—will read every shred of graffiti on their way to the refrigerator or while talking on the telephone.

2. Subscribe to publications from groups working for nonviolent social change, such as *The Nonviolent Activist*, advocating a halt and resistance to the nuclear arms race; or *Greenpeace*, about protecting the environment.

3. Keep a collection box at the center of the kitchen table, marked "Bread for the World," "Oxfam America," or "Sane/ Freeze," not only for the occasional donations from other parents, children, and visitors, but also for the questions it may provoke about what the organization stands for and why. Change it every few months to keep the issues current.

4. Ask the local spokesperson of a particular organization— Mobilization for Survival, Committee in Solidarity with the People of El Salvador, or another—to your home so that the children will not only "take in" information, but also begin to associate movements for peace and justice with particular people.

5. Invite the neighborhood, including children, to discussions, films, or events focusing on global issues. Trick or Treat for UNICEF at Halloween. UNICEF greeting cards for Christmas have long been a useful means of encouraging international awareness in our city. Whenever possible, combine education and festivities, through religious liturgies, concerts, art exhibits, fairs, and poetry readings.

6. Involve the family in supporting local charities and groups—women's shelters, soup kitchens, interfaith peace com-

mittees — in whatever way seems appropriate. No person can do everything (there is, in fact, a danger of burn-out if we overextend ourselves, particularly at the expense of time with our children); but everyone can make a contribution: by writing letters of support, donating money (or in-kind contributions), or assisting others similarly involved.

7. Ask children, or simply take them along, if they have no objections, to public gatherings about important social issues: town meetings, debates, vigils, demonstrations, where they will see and gain a feeling for democracy at work. Recommend and support their participation in activities associated with governance and gaining control of their own lives.

COMMUNITY SUPPORT GROUPS

Persons or families committed to global values need the support and encouragement of a wider community. In many cities and towns through the United States, that community must be built, sometimes from the ground up. In others, parents simply need to rely on resources already available, in the long process of community education.

Individual or family efforts might include helping to plan public vigils or providing child care for other parents involved in active resistance at nuclear testing sites and arms manufacturers (such as those sponsored annually by Pax Christi USA, Clamshell Alliance, or Beyond War). Building community means performing simple tasks faithfully and persistently. As Dr. Helen Caldicott, a major force in developing awareness around nuclear issues has reminded us, social change can be accomplished by anyone, even without previous experience. "The momentum for movement [to abolish nuclear weapons] can only originate in the heart and mind of the individual citizen," she said. "Moreover, it takes only one person to initiate the process, and that person may be politically naive and inexperienced, just as I was when I first spoke out."

The movement to stop the next weapons system begins at a ward or town meeting rather than in the halls of Congress. "Never doubt that a small group of thoughtful, committed citizens can change the world," the anthropologist Margaret Mead once said; "indeed, it's the only thing that ever has." In this context, a father or mother becomes "our own secretary of state," in helping to build what someone has called "municipal foreign policies," not waiting for the president to sign a bill or for Congress to pass a law. Recent examples of such citizen diplomacy include: (1) establishing sister city relationships with communities in the Soviet Union and Central American (for example, Worcester, Massachusetts, with Pushkin, U.S.S.R., and Comalpa, Nicaragua); (2) declaring nuclear-free zones that keep out nuclear weapons manufacturers and nuclear waste (Cambridge, Massachusetts, and the State of Vermont); (3) supporting peace studies courses in the school systems (Milwaukee and the State of Ohio; the Martin Luther King Center in Atlanta and the Martin Luther King Institute in Albany, New York, to name a few).

Although some groups emerge quickly around common concerns, most are built over time through hard work, and nourished through a positive spirit of a small group of activists. No community forms around "gloom and doom"; and one should never undervalue simple signs of hospitality associated with private conversations over coffee or a common meal. People often join efforts to alter the priorities of their town or national government because they feel alienated and alone, so one must make a special point to listen to others, as well as to name one's own grievances against, or hopes for, the social order.

"The democratic challenge for the new century," as Richard J. Barnet has said, "is to build communities in which all people are needed, wanted, and honored." If parents practice these values in the home, they will naturally spill over into the world outside. The spiritual wounds, represented by the crushing problems that divide Americans—racism, drugs, and poverty—can be healed not by denial, "which works no better in the United States than it does in the Soviet Union [or China], but by the determination of the people to make democracy work."

In all of these efforts, I must repeat, communities that matter usually begin very modestly, sometimes with ten or fewer people who are fully committed to the communal tasks. Communities of people with ideals, such as those committed to creating a space for "invisible" people or to recognizing the importance of "unimportant" people, almost always begin tentatively, under pressure. They take root in spite of, and in resistance to, the dominant culture, represented by wealthy and powerful organizations: government agencies, churches, multinational businesses, and universities that sometimes cavort with "the whole rotten system," as Dorothy Day used to call it.

Although peace and justice groups almost inevitably come into conflict with institutions of power and prestige, the latter can be helpful, nonetheless, in the struggle, as long as we don't waste our energy giving them more attention than they deserve, and as long as we endeavour, on occasion, to free ourselves from their dominance. Schools and colleges, for example, through courses and activities are essential to peace education; but in the face of budget cuts or the usual bureaucratic hassles, they forget their way. So parents cannot depend upon them to provide leadership and continuity on justice issues. School systems and large universities are particularly susceptible to reigning ideologies of the moment, and regularly grind up people in lusting for prestige and government support. Beware of the state and its wars on poverty or drugs or anything else.

Children, of course, have a hard time learning these distinctions, and parents must maintain a kind of constant juggling act helping them to understand. Large institutions and public and private agencies contribute to the general welfare by building roads, preserving order, maintaining forests and beaches, building parks, and generally helping to make our lives secure. The same institutions, however, sometimes discriminate against or exclude people, judging them acceptable or unacceptable on the basis of distorted priorities; they finance and build nuclear weapons and, through the disbursement of funds, penalize the poor and minorities, while protecting the wealth and power of a select few.

●

In the 1990s, people are perhaps more aware of the relationship between injustice and social structures than at any time since the 1930s. The principal reason for this change is their growing concern about the environment—the earth in all its abundance and variety. Parents who might otherwise pay little attention to the Pentagon's budget regarding the shipment of arms to Third World countries, for example, have begun to attend to that budget when the Pentagon is singled out as a major polluter of water supplies across the country.

People challenging the conventional wisdom about the dangers of nuclear energy and nuclear weapons, and abuses of basic human rights, have increased our awareness and shown us new ways of being good citizens. Had it not been for the Atlantic and Pacific Life communities, for example, we might never have learned about the harmful effects of radiation and other dangers faced by workers in nuclear power plants. Similarly, groups such as Amnesty International and America Watch and journalists such as the late Penny Lernoux regularly have exposed human rights abuses in China, Guatemala, Brazil, and the Middle East.

Today, many people are in closer touch with agents for social change than they were twenty years ago. In every region of the United States, these agencies are visible, addressing issues such as the proliferation of nuclear weapons, the need for a new foreign policy toward Latin America, the care of the environment, and support for people deprived of basic human rights and necessities.

I see another sign of hope in the increasing number of publications, including children's books, that dramatize the importance of these issues and suggest the power of people in community to gain control over forces formerly left to "the experts." Among many publications on this theme, usually available at the public library, for every age level, I shall mention a few representative ones.

A Children's Chorus (New York: E. P. Dutton, 1989), for example, sets the ten principles of the U.N. General Assembly's Declaration of the Rights of the Child beside beautiful illustrations of how those rights apply in everyday life. Audrey Hepburn recommends it, accurately, as a book "for children to look at; to share with a brother, a sister, parent, teacher or friend; to laugh and to learn the joy that should belong to every child." For children ten and older, *Dreams of a Perfect Earth* (New York: Atheneum, 1982), by Lorus J. and Margery Milne, discusses ecological systems, with questions about the reader's neighborhood, town, or city.

A series published by Values Communications, Inc., La Jolla, California, recommends a particular social value by telling the story of a remarkable person, as these two titles suggest: Ann Donegan Johnson, *The Value of Friendship: Jane Addams* (1979); Spencer Johnson, *The Value of Dedication: Albert Schweitzer* (1979). William Penn, Lucretia Mott, and Harriet Tubman are other community builders included in this "value" series, with well-told tales, colorful illustrations, and brief biographical factsheets. Like the biographies of peacemakers mentioned in the appendix, these stories emphasize the relationship between individual effort and the common good.

Even though a kind of individualistic, know-nothing social ethic ("the politics of greed") has shaped foreign and domestic policy during the Reagan/Bush administrations, a sizable minority of people has begun to behave as if it knows and understands how a democractic society is supposed to work. When one person — or more — stands against injustice or for the welfare of others, communities form around him or her; conversely, where communities of concerned citizens take action, individuals are more willing to take the risks necessary to bring a just society into being.

A dramatic example of the mutual benefit of citizen action to the individual and the community is evident in the person of Brian Willson. A member of Veterans Peace Action Teams, he lost his legs when a train ran over him at the Concord, California, Naval Weapons Station, as he blocked the shipment of nuclear weapons. "Ironically, I now have more 'standing' as a peace wager than I had before . . . and millions of friends around the world," he wrote in 1987. "The experience of standing up to the death train and wondering what my survival means has left me with a metaphysical and spiritual consciousness beyond my capacity to put in words. I am more liberated than ever to share the gift of life, . . . more committed than ever to wage unconditional peace with the empowering force of nonviolence."

Acquainting ourselves and our children with such people, as well as with the resources for education and action on nonviolence (also listed in the appendix), is a way of helping the best communal values in our culture flourish.

A CAUTIONARY NOTE

Whatever activities that a parent asks a child to participate in, in the home or community, he or she does well to tailor such events to a child's age and disposition, never overextending or burdening a youngster beyond his or her physical or emotional capacity. In addition, a parent teaching social values must try to accept whatever response the child offers, positive or negative, however insignificant it seems. Attitudes change, so even criticism suggests interest, sometimes, on the way to involvement.

In all activities associated with developing a social conscience, parents must remember that the purpose of them is to develop awareness, *not* to seek agreement; and parents must be prepared for a child's testing them every step of the way, sometimes at the most awkward moment and in unexpected ways.

In bringing public issues to children's attention, parents may be asking them to commit themselves to issues that friends and classmates, even teachers, regard as irrelevant or unpopular or—worst of all, for some—"controversial." So parents should never make children's agreeing with them a condition for respecting their point of view.

Whatever else is recommended about teaching social values to children in this book, a parent's unconditional love, in any hierarchy of values, is always paramount. (One way of reminding children of that fact, by the way, is to read, with them, Margaret Wise Brown's beautiful story, *The Runaway Bunny* [New York: Harper and Row, 1972].)

Being able to count on their parents' love is, after all, essential if children are to learn to trust themselves, take their place in the larger community, and become "citizens of the world."

PART IV

CONCLUSION

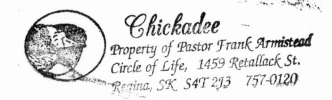

9

BEING CITIZENS
OF THE WORLD

We're bound to each other
with unknown thread, a stitch
of red corpuscles sewing up the globe.
— Piotr Summer

In "The Mouse Roulette Wheel," a story by Carol Bly, Father
Bill Hewlitt, a forty-one-year-old Episcopal priest in a small
Minnesota town, faces two decisions with moral implications for
his family and the community. Early one morning, as parishioners and townspeople arrive and prepare for the annual church
fair, Father Hewlitt must decide, first of all, how he will respond
to the protest by several young parishioners who regard using
mice at a gambling table as being cruel to animals. Will he agree
to close the game down? Father Hewlitt and his wife must also
decide whether they will accept an inheritance from his brother,
a former government official with CIA connections, who has
recently come home to die.

The young curate eventually sides with the children and
closes down the mouse roulette wheel; also, even though they
have no chance to talk beforehand, he and his wife say to his
brother that they cannot accept the million dollar inheritance,

although it would provide needed funds for their sons' college educations.

The following morning, during his Sunday sermon, Father Hewlitt says that human beings making choices "have to consider on absolutely every occasion, 'Who's *invisible* in the scene?'" Hesitantly, thinking that his words might sound harsh to parishioners who make money off local strip mining or to one parishioner who earlier informed on students for the CIA, he adds: "Even if we get paid just to change the towels every morning for an organization that is cruel, it still means . . . we aren't *keeping* our invisible brother properly."

This story dramatizes a conflict each of us faces, in different ways, in our efforts to live responsibly. As Father Hewlitt says, the dilemma is often posed as a question: Who might be hurt by a decision we make or an action we take, as parents, children, voters, citizens?

Almost any day, the morning paper raises this question again, regarding the poor of this country or abroad who face further victimization as a result of U.S. domestic or foreign policy (anyone living in Japan or Germany or France or any other wealthy, industrialized country obviously faces a similar condition). Recently, for example, two congressmen from my state voted to approve another $400 million in U.S. aid to the military government of El Salvador, after seventy thousand people have been killed. They did so even after the film *Romero* and an earlier biography reminded us that the martyred archbishop of San Salvador pleaded with the United States in 1980 to stop arming the military regime there. How am I, as an American voter, to respond to this injustice? How can I make visible the suffering of those who are "invisible" to legislators, with powers over life and death in their hands? How might I suggest to my children that being responsible human beings involves "pledging allegiance to the victims," as Albert Camus once said?

Keeping "invisible" people in mind is related to what William Lloyd Garrison, the nineteenth-century abolitionist, meant in calling himself "a citizen of the world." Being that kind of American citizen in the late twentieth century means keeping in mind the following paradigm:

If the entire world consisted of 100 people:
   67 would be poor.
   55 would have an annual income of less than $600.
   50 would be homeless or live in substandard housing.
   50 would be without adequate, safe drinking water.
   47 would be illiterate.
   35 would be hungry and malnourished.
   6 would be Americans and would hold 33 percent of
      the world's income.
   1 would have a college education.

One keeps these facts at some level of consciousness not out of shame or guilt, but out of a wish to be aware of the world in which he or she lives. One does so in order to remember the millions of people whose security — even survival — may depend upon the values we live by and teach our children.

Since World War II, many people outside this country have become "invisible" to the American people, just as minorities and the poor become increasingly "invisible" in our own country. As the propaganda war of the Cold War raged, we took to regarding citizens of other countries as "good guys" or "bad guys," depending upon how loyal they appeared to be to the economic and military interests of the United States. In this ideological struggle, other cultures "disappeared" from public consciousness, particularly if they steadfastly resisted any attempt to enlist them in the ideological struggle between the United States and the U.S.S.R. Worse, the people of various countries, in particular decades, were treated by the popular media as people of another planet. The most blatant example of negative image-making occurred when President Reagan referred to the U.S.S.R. as "the evil empire," but along with that we were indoctrinated to "hate" the Chinese or the Iranians or the Nicaraguans or whoever else challenged State policy at the moment.

There are complex psychological forces that undermine our inclination to behave as citizens in the tradition of Paine and Garrison. Part of the explanation may lie in our failure to come to terms with the grief and pain that many endured as a result of the Vietnam War. Perhaps our fear of nuclear war, our confusion over the destruction of community ties, and the highly individualistic ethic of "each against all" contributed to our change of attitude. Whatever the case, people's natural feelings of worldwide interdependence gave way. And for a while, whole areas of the globe simply disappeared from view.

Periodically, in order to justify U.S. military intervention, in Southeast Asia, then the Middle East, then Latin America, political propaganda succeeded in convincing much of the American public that certain foreign peoples were simply not "human" in the same way we are. In her beautiful memoir of her ancestry and visits to Czechoslovakia, *A Romantic Education*, Patricia Hampl describes how for many years Central Europe simply did not exist for many Americans. Because of its relative unimportance to the Cold War, that area of the world disappeared from view, until the 1980s, when people in that region began risking their necks and adopting political attitudes sympathetic to the West.

Increasingly, however, these stereotypes have broken down. One agent for change is the effort of various groups—such as Cultural Survival, Inc., Physicians for Social Responsibility, and Promoting Enduring Peace—to counter stereotypes and mind games perpetuated by the media. In meetings sponsored by the Center for the Study of the Psychological Effects of Nuclear War, for example, filmmakers from the United States and the U.S.S.R. examined the caricatures they often relied upon in representing the people of "the other country." To undo the psychological damage of such stereotypes, parents need to help children to see the people of other countries as human beings with wishes, hopes, sufferings, and joys similar to their own.

MAKING ROOM FOR ALL THE PEOPLE OF THE EARTH

This effort at world citizenship begins by parents encouraging children to make that leap of imagination so essential to an understanding of others. It is accomplished only with the greatest effort, not because children are innately suspicious of other races or nationalities—for the most part they are not—but because of the cultural biases that permeate the culture of the

United States (and many other cultures) in subtle and not so subtle ways. Since nationalism and racism often poison relationships among citizens within this country, it is not surprising that they also influence attitudes toward people living distant from our shores.

How can we teach that all people deserve enough to eat, as well as clothing and shelter, simply because they are human? How might parents convey a respect for basic human rights, agreed upon by all countries in the United Nations almost fifty years ago? One basic step, as I suggested in chapter 6, is to convey a sense of the sacredness of life and to encourage a compassion for (literally, *feeling with*) others, through association with children of other nations. Another basic step is helping children develop that powerful muscle, the imagination, strengthened and toned by folk tales, stories, and poems (by Dr. Seuss, E. B. White, Maurice Sendak, etc.). Another step is learning poems and stories that suggest the values of other cultures, such as the following one by an eleven-year-old Italian girl, Anna Soldi, entitled "A Heart Made of Bread":

> I saw at the baker's a heart made of bread,
> big, hot and fragrant and I thought:
> "If I had a heart of bread,
> how many children could eat?
> For you, my friend, who are hungry,
> for you a mouthful of my heart's bread.
> And for you, and for you, and for you."
> It's not enough to say "I love you"
> to a child who's hungry and scared.
> It's not enough to say "poor mite"
> if you see a child in tears.
> If my heart was made of bread,
> how many children could eat!
> And you who are in command,
> what's keeping you back,
> why don't you make bombs of bread?
> At the end of the battle each soldier
> joyfully would take back home
> a basket of golden bombs fragrant and crusty.

But this is a dream,
and my hungry friend is still in tears.
If only my heart was made of bread!

WHAT IS TO BE DONE?

Appreciating the value of other cultures might encourage us to behave as good citizens in working for certain priorities in our own country and the rest of the world.

One person or one family cannot and obviously should not even try to address all the issues. Beginning with one issue, however, such as that related to world hunger, will put families in touch with communities of people working to alleviate various social ills, as the poem by the young Italian symbolically suggests.

Seeing that every person on the earth has food is not an unrealistic goal, as several commentators have argued, since the world produces enough for everyone's survival. The current yield, for example, would feed the projected world population of six billion people for the year 2000. Since "poverty, not scarcity or natural disasters, is the root cause of the majority of hunger-related deaths, there *are* solutions available," according to an important documentary on "the politics of food." In this, as in other areas of "making peace," parents can do a great deal in strengthening their own and their children's determination to create a new climate of opinion and to initiate a new course of action on all peace and justice issues.

The first move is to make, perhaps, a leap of faith, committing ourselves to new "habits of the heart," and bringing ourselves closer to the values recommended by all the great religions: love, reverence for human life and the natural universe, and resistance to exploitation and injustice. "All things are connected like the blood which unites one family," as Chief Seattle said a century ago. "All things are connected."

As long as social values remain peripheral rather than central convictions of our lives, the disorder in our world will increase. Honoring them means, at some level, acquiring an ethical worldview and teaching it to our children.

•

Teaching global values to children, in a culture dominated by nationalism and chauvinism, takes energy, imagination, and courage. It is now, as before, a worthy task, one that keeps a parent attentive and humble. Since such a commitment inevitably puts one in conflict, occasionally with one's neighbors and associates, it may also prove rather trying.

On the basis of thirty years of experience, nonetheless, I recommend it. For the home is a good place "for both envisioning and working on everyday realities for a better future," as Elise Boulding has suggested: "Not the only place, but a good place." And if we're doing it right, we will find ourselves increasingly aligned with the victims of the world. The fact that these values and activities associated with them put us in conflict, occasionally, with principalities and powers, kings and princes, presidents and magistrates, may be the first sign that we are on the right track. In fulfilling our responsibility to our children and to others, these words of John Henry Newman, the great Victorian clergyman and writer, suggest the spirit we might wish to cultivate in living values somewhat different from those that have characterized American public life in recent decades: "In necessary things unity, in doubtful things liberty, and in all things charity."

At the same time, parents need to keep their attention focused and priorities clearly in mind, including a family's will to resist many of the inane practices that perpetuate the violence of the status quo. So we must keep learning, reading, and welcoming opportunities for clarification of thought. Everyone, as Gandhi said, must have a text to refer to, and throughout this book I have made reference to several that have helped to sustain various parents over the years. Such texts almost inevitably repeat the wish—a kind of prayer, really—of the forgiving son in Stanley Kunitz's poem "Father and Son." "Instruct your son," he says to his father (or Father),

> For I would be a child to those who mourn
> And brother to the foundlings of the field

And friend of innocence and all bright eyes.
O teach me how to work and keep me kind.

Among the many religious and secular writings that I have turned to over the years, the essays of Paul Goodman, American poet, pamphleteer, and war resister, have been particularly sustaining. I remember particularly his address to the National Security Industrial Association—"a wealthy club" of government advisers and multinational corporations that account for much of the research and development in the military/industrial/university complex. Speaking in Washington, D.C., in 1967, Goodman offered its members two choices: (1) initiate a program with three essential goals: reviving American democracy, rescuing the majority of humankind from deepening poverty, and insuring humanity's survival as a species; *or* (2) disband.

Goodman said the three goals mentioned in the first choice require research and experimentation of the highest sophistication, but not by people unfit for the task by their commitments, experience, methods, and moral disposition. Goodman continued:

> You are the military industrial of the United States, the most dangerous body of men at present in the world, for you not only implement our disastrous policies but are an overwhelming lobby for them, and you expand and rigidify the wrong use of brains, resources, and labor so that change becomes difficult. Most likely the trends you represent will be interrupted by a shambles of riots, alienation, ecological catastrophes, wars, and revolutions.... [and] the best service that you people could perform is rather rapidly to phase yourselves out, passing on your relevant knowledge to people better qualified, or reorganizing yourselves with entirely different sponsors and commitments, so that you learn to think and feel in a different way. Since you are most of the [research and development] that there is, we cannot do without you as people, but we cannot do with you as you are.

One wishes that the military/industrial/university complex had taken Goodman's advice in 1967, but alas it did not, and the consequences—"riots, alienation, ecological catastrophes, wars, and revolutions"—are pretty much as he described them. As a rallying cry, Goodman's speech is still relevant in alerting parents to their responsibilities in the future. In his other writings, such as his lively, readable essay on city planning, "Communitas," Goodman described a community that places social values and a strong civic culture at the center of its life and activity. In identifying our task for the immediate future, one might add Thomas Berry's principle of "activating the intercommunion of all the living and non-living components of the earth community."

In homes permeated by values associated with social justice, parents can make a difference. Against the heavy rhetoric of violence and greed, justifying nuclear weapons and victimization of the world's poor, we can speak a language with a different syntax, a new grammar. As Denise Levertov says in "Making Peace" (mentioned earlier), we can create "an energy field more intense than war, ... each act of living / one of its words, each word / a vibration of light—facets / of a forming crystal."

Sometimes risky, often difficult, occasionally joyous, rearing children is a noble task, a great vocation, as they drag us, kicking and screaming, into their world. There we are called to mediate between the dominant culture and an alternative culture. There we are called to uphold values reflecting the best traditions available from our own culture and from other cultures of the world.

APPENDIX

A NOTE ON FAMILY RESOURCES

Since children grow into reading habits as they develop new learning habits, parents are wise to make sure that good newspapers, magazines, and books are easily accessible to them. Even if they don't read the publications regularly, children attend to what their parents read and inevitably rely on what is easily available for school assignments; gradually, they develop a sense of writers and publications that are or are not informed on public issues.

Inexpensive periodicals and materials for the home are easily accessible, if one knows where to look for them. But parents cannot expect "the best that is known and thought in the world" to fall into their laps. And it is naive to expect that watching the evening news or reading popular magazines will provide the kind of thoughtful, informed reporting essential to an informed citizenry. As Michael Deaver, one of President Reagan's key advisers, admitted, White House publicists regard television reporters not as serious journalists, but as members of the entertainment industry. Parents should treat most television reporting in a similar manner. News coverage on National Public Radio and educational television stations is, on the other hand, often well informed. Also, since local and regional stations and publications may provide thoughtful reporting and commentary, no source of information should be ignored in our effort to remain well informed.

Among the many accessible sources of information for parents and children, the following items—in addition to those already mentioned in the text—provide a good introduction.

NEWSPAPERS AND MAGAZINES

Three relatively inexpensive periodicals that focus on justice issues, with attractive graphics, as well as clear, informed prose are (1) *Maryknoll*, Maryknoll, NY 10545 (monthly; voluntary contribution); (2) *Catholic Worker*, 36 East First Street, New York, NY 10003 (monthly; 25¢ a year); (3) *Sojourners*, P.O. Box 29272, Washington, DC 20077 (monthly; $24 a year).

Local newspapers, even in larger cities, are notoriously deficient in providing adequate international news, particularly perspectives other than those based upon White House press releases. Several journals of opinion, however, regularly publish excellent writers for whom social justice is something more than a catch phrase; they include *Atlantic, Christian Science Monitor, Commonweal, Harper's, The Nation, The New Yorker, New York Review of Books,* and *The Progressive.*

Alternative newspapers in various regions of the United States, some of them distributed free of charge, sometimes provide informed news coverage, as do several newsletters; *Peacework: A New England Peace and Social Justice Newsletter*, in Massachusetts, and *Active for Justice: A Voice for Social Justice and Nonviolence,* in Colorado, for example, publish articles and list events related to justice and peace education in their regions.

Reprints of articles from alternative publications appear regularly in *Utne Reader: The Best of the Alternative Press*, a bimonthly journal published from The Fawkes Building, 1624 Harmon Place, Minneapolis, MN 55403, and distributed nationally; a representative issue centered on the theme "Paradise Found: How the Environmental Crisis Can *Improve* Our Lives" (November-December 1989). Reprints of brief articles on peace issues are also available *free of charge* from Promoting Enduring Peace, Inc. ("a non-profit, non-political group of religious and educational opportunities"), P.O. Box 5103, Woodmont, CT 06460.

BOOKS

As children move into the school years, they need authoritative histories—for information, encouragement, and inspiration—about how a peaceful society is built and how injustices are corrected. Like adults, children like to hear stories about people who, though flawed and inconsistent, remained faithful and responsible to the welfare of the community, in the past or present.

Among a host of suitable biographies for young people about heroes and heroines of social justice, the following are attractive and readable, usually for children eight and older. Sharman Apt Russell's *Frederick Douglass* (New York: Chelsea House, 1988) is one of a series of illustrated biographies about "Black Americans of Achievement," including Sojourner Truth, Harriet Tubman, and Martin Luther King. Books of similar quality include James P. Terzian and Kathryn Cramer, *Mighty Hard Road: The Story of Cesar Chavez* (Garden City, N.Y.: Doubleday and Co., 1970); Jeannette Eaton, *Gandhi: Fighter without a Sword* (New York: William Morrow, 1950); Linda Atkinson, *Mother Jones: The Most Dangerous Woman in America* (New York: Crown Publishers, 1978).

At some point, children become curious about specific episodes in American history: when people initiated grassroots efforts and large campaigns to win rights for workers and women, to resist the draft, nuclear armaments, and oppression, and to protect endangered species and the natural environment.

For young and older adults, here are five authoritative, readable guides to nonviolent movements for social change in the United States, with bibliographies on particular movements and individuals: (1) Charles DeBenedetti, *The Peace Reform in American History* (Bloomington: Indiana University Press, 1980); (2) Staughton Lynd, ed., *Nonviolence in America: A Documentary History* (Indianapolis: Bobbs-Merrill, 1968); (3) Robert Cooney and Helen Michalowski, eds., *The Power of the People: Active Nonviolence in the United States* (Philadelphia: New Society Publishers, 1987); (4) Michael True, *Justice-Seekers, Peacemakers: 32 Portraits in Courage* (Mystic, CT: Twenty-Third Publications, 1985); (5) Howard Zinn, *People's History of the United States* (New York: Harper and Row, 1980).

Two important reference works discussing similar movements throughout the world, as well as Nobel Prize laureates for peace, are (1) Ervin Laszlo and Jong Youl Yoo, eds., *World Encyclopedia of Peace*, 4 vols. (Exeter, England: Pergamon Press, 1986); and (2) Alan J. Day, ed., *Peace Movements of the World: An International Directory* (Essex, England: Longman, 1986). A useful guide to academic programs, when children begin thinking about colleges and universities, is Daniel C. Thomas and Michael T. Klare, *Peace and World Order Studies*, 5th ed. (Boulder, CO: Westview Press, 1989). All the above books belong, obviously, in school and public libraries.

Also, *never* underestimate the skills and imagination of *your local librarian*, regarding books, journals, and materials essential to the education of your children, at various ages and ability. Particularly if they are parents, librarians are often well acquainted with biographies and other nonfiction about justice-seekers and peacemakers who will interest children, and —*perhaps more importantly* —with folk tales, poetry, fiction, and drama that "teach" moral values in the most artful, memorable, imaginative, and entertaining way. Librarians are usually familiar, also, with local figures who by example or in their writings address social issues of the past or present.

FILMS AND VIDEOS

There are many guides to films and videos about social values, for general use at home, in school, church, or community centers, including *Catalog of Audio-Visual Materials*, available from the Nuclear Age Resource Center, Cuyahoga Community Center, 4250 Richmond Road, Cleveland, OH 44122. Others are easily obtainable through a local library, college, university, or peace center library.

Among the many video rentals (usually VHS, 10–30 minutes in length, at $5, plus shipping), the following are representative: (1) *Beginning with the Children*, produced by Educators for Social

Responsibility, on resolving conflict in the classroom and on the playground; (2) *Buster and Me: Getting Active*, a muppet presentation about sharing fears and taking action around the issue of nuclear war; (3) *Fighting Fair: Dr. Martin Luther King, Jr., for Kids*, about a coach helping children resolve a conflict on the basketball court; (4) *Growing Up with the Bomb*, from the "20/ 20" news magazine, with psychologists Dr. William Beardslee and Dr. John Mack, on children helping other children face their fears about nuclear destruction.

Documentaries and feature-length films appropriate for older children and easily accessible include *Eyes on the Prize*, parts 1 and 2, on the civil rights movement; *Gandhi*, centering on his public life and the struggle for independence; *Dorothy Day: Still a Rebel*, an interview with Bill Moyers; and *Romero*, about the last years of the late archbishop of San Salvador.

SOME USEFUL ADDRESSES

State governments in Iowa and Ohio have established centers for peace education and conflict resolution, with materials for exhibition and publication. Information on these and related educational ventures appears in the bi-monthly *COPRED Peace Chronicle*, published by the Consortium on Peace Research, Education and Development, George Mason University, 4400 University Drive, Fairfax, VA 22030.

Parenting for Peace and Justice Network, Institute for Peace and Justice, 4144 Lindell, #400, St. Louis, MO 63108, provides a useful newsletter, valuable workshop materials, and services for family support groups, including brief guidelines for conducting family meetings, church camps, and other communal efforts. Specific information for younger peacemakers appears in *Peace "Works,"* published by The Grace Contrino Abrams Peace Education Foundation, Inc., 3550 Biscayne Boulevard., Suite 400, Miami, FL 33137.

Two important resources for the study of nonviolence are the Martin Luther King, Jr., Center for Social Change, 449 Auburn Avenue, N.E., Atlanta, GA 30312, and the New York State Martin Luther King, Jr., Institute for Nonviolence, 41 State Street, Albany, NY 12201. The United States Institute of Peace, 1550 M Street, N.W., Suite 700, Washington, DC 20005—primarily a funding organization to support the study of war, peace, and international conflict — publishes transcripts of discussions on peace issues.

Many peace and environmental organizations publish colorful booklets, graphics, and games suitable for children, as well as manuals for parents and teachers about developing skills for conflict resolution and living in a global society (see, for example, Ruth Fletcher, *Teaching Peace*, and Stephanie Judson, ed., *A Manual on Nonviolence and Children*, listed in the bibliography below). Beautiful maps (specific to a child's particular interest or choice), videos, books, games, and toys related to all aspects of planet earth are available through the U.S. Committee for UNICEF, 475 Oberlin Avenue So., CN2110, Lakewood, NJ 08701, and National Geographic Society, 17th and M Streets, N. W., Washington, DC 20036.

A comprehensive list of U.S. organizations devoted to nonviolent social change appears in *The Power of the People* (listed above), pp. 262–63, including these seven well-known groups, some with local and regional chapters or organizers:

1. A. J. Muste Institute
   339 Lafayette Street
   New York, NY 10012
2. American Friends Service Committee
   1501 Cherry Street
   Philadelphia, PA 19102
3. Pax Christi USA
   348 East Tenth Street
   Erie, PA 16503
4. Fellowship of Reconciliation
   P.O. Box 271
   Nyack, NY 10960
5. Union of Concerned Scientists
   26 Church Street
   Cambridge, MA 02138
6. Sierra Club
   730 Polk Street
   San Francisco, CA 94109
7. Educators for Social Responsibility
   23 Garden Street
   Cambridge, MA 02138

BIBLIOGRAPHY

Ashbrook, Tom. "Back in the USA." *Boston Globe Magazine*, February 19, 1989.

Barnet, Richard J. "The Challenge of Change: U.S. Foreign Policy at the Start of a New Decade." *Sojourners* 18, no. 6 (June 1989): 14–18.

Bellah, Robert N., et al. *Habits of the Heart: Individualism and Commitment in American Life*. New York: Harper and Row, 1985.

Bennett, Jon. *The Hunger Machine*. New York: Polity Press/Basil Blackwell, 1987.

Berrigan, Daniel. *Daniel Berrigan: Poetry, Drama, Prose*. Ed. Michael True. Maryknoll, N.Y.: Orbis Books, 1988.

Berrigan, Philip, and Elizabeth McAlister. *The Time's Discipline: The Beatitudes and Nuclear Resistance*. Baltimore: Fortkamp Publishing Co., 1989.

Berry, Wendell. "The Futility of Global Thinking." *Harper's* 279, no. 1672 (September 1989): 16–19, 22.

Bly, Carol. *Backbone*. Minneapolis: Milkweed Editions, 1985.

———. *Letters from the Country*. New York: Harper and Row, 1981.

———. ed. *Everybody's Story: An Anthology of Writing by Older Minnesotans*. St. Paul: COMPAS Literary Post, 1987.

Bly, Robert. *The Light around the Body*. New York: Harper and Row, 1967.

Boff, Leonardo. *Jesus Christ Liberator: A Critical Christology for Our Time*. Maryknoll, N.Y.: Orbis Books, 1978.

Boulding, Elise. *Building a Global Civic Culture: Education for an Interdependent World*. New York: Teachers College Press, 1988.

———. *One Small Plot of Heaven: Reflections of Family Life by a Quaker Sociologist*. Wallingford, Pa.: Pendel Hill Publications, 1989.

Boulding, Kenneth. *Stable Peace*. Austin: University of Texas Press, 1978.

Brodsky, Joseph. *Less Than One: Selected Essays*. New York: Farrar, Straus and Giroux, 1986.

Brown, Robert McAfee. *National Catholic Reporter*, April 8, 1983.

Caduto, Michael J., and Joseph Bruchac. *Keepers of the Earth: Native American Stories and Environmental Activities for Children*. Golden, Colo.: Fulcrum, Inc., 1988.

Cathy, S., A. Gurwitz, and J. M. Ross. *Father and Child: Clinical and Developmental Considerations* Boston: Little, Brown, 1982.

Clark, Eric. *The Want Makers: The World of Advertising: How They Make You Buy*. New York: Viking, 1989.

Clark, Mary E. *Ariadne's Thread: The Search for New Modes of Thinking*. New York: St. Martin's, 1989.

Coles, Robert. *The Political Life of Children*. Boston: Houghton Mifflin, 1986.

Damon, William. *The Moral Child: Nurturing Children's Natural Moral Growth*. New York: The Free Press, 1988.

Donovan, Vincent J. *The Church in the Midst of Creation*. Maryknoll, N.Y.: Orbis Books, 1989.

Dyson, Freeman. *Weapons and Hope*. New York: Harper and Row, 1984.

Emerson, Gloria. *Some American Men*. New York: Simon and Schuster, 1985.

Everett, Melissa. *Breaking Ranks*. Philadelphia: New Society Publishers, 1989.

Fletcher, Ruth. *Teaching Peace*. San Francisco: Harper and Row, 1986.

Freudenberger, Herbert J. "Today's Troubled Men." *Psychology Today* (December 1987): 46–47.

Gagnon, Paul. "Why Study History?" *Atlantic* 262, no. 5 (November 1988): 43–46, 50–66.

Glenn, John H. "The Mini-Hiroshima Near Cincinnati." *New York Times*, January 24, 1989.

Goodman, Ellen. "Try a Little Drug-Healing Instead of War." *Boston Globe*, September 12, 1989.

———. "When the Moral Life of Children Jabs at Adults." *Boston Globe*, October 17, 1989.

Goodman, Paul. *Drawing the Line: Political Essays*. Ed. Taylor Stoehr. New York: Free Life Editions, 1977.

Gordon, Thomas. *P.E.T. Parent Effectiveness Training: The Tested New Way To Raise Responsible Children*. New York: Peter H. Wyden, 1970.

Hatfield, Mark O. "Peace through Strength Is a Fallacy . . . " *Congressional Record* 135, no. 107 (August 2, 1989).

Hauerwas, Stanley. "Peacemaking Is Conflict-making." *Expressions: St. Benedict Center* (September-October 1989): 1–2, 8.

Hick, John, and Paul F. Knitter, eds. *The Myth of Christian Uniqueness: Toward a Pluralistic Theology of Religions*. Maryknoll, N.Y.: Orbis Books, 1987.

Judson, Stephanie, ed., *A Manual on Nonviolence and Children*. Philadelphia: New Society Publishers, 1984.

Juergensmeyer, Mark. *Fighting Fair: A Non-violent Strategy for Resolving Everyday Conflicts*. New York: Harper and Row, 1986.

King, Martin Luther, Jr. *Loving Your Enemies, Letter from Birmingham Jail, and Declaration of Independence from the War in Vietnam*. New York: A. J. Muste Memorial Institute Essay Series, no. 1, n.d..

Kitwood, Tom. *Concern for Others: A New Psychology of Conscience and Morality*. London: Routledge, 1990.

Kizer, Carolyn. "The Worms," *Midnight Was My Cry: New and Selected Poems*. Garden City, N.Y.: Doubleday, 1971.

Kohlberg, Lawrence. *The Philosophy of Moral Development*. San Francisco: Harper and Row, 1981.

Kome, Penney, and Patrick Crean. *Peace: A Dream Unfolding*. San Francisco: Sierra Club Books, 1986.

Küng, Hans. *Theology for the Third Millennium: An Ecumenical View*. New York: Doubleday, 1988.

Kunitz, Stanley. "The Poet's Quest for the Father." *New York Times Book Review*, February 22, 1987.

Lerner, Michael. "Looking Forward to the Nineties." *Tikkun* (November-December 1989): 37–41.

Levertov, Denise. "Making Peace." In *Breathing the Water*. New York: New Directions, 1986, 40.

———. "Political Action in Which Each Individual Acts from the Heart." In *Candles in Babylon*. New York: New Directions, 1982, 86.

Lifton, Robert Jay, and Richard Falk. *Indefensible Weapons: The Political and Psychological Case against Nuclearism*. New York: Basic Books, 1982.

McGinnis, Kathleen, and James McGinnis. *Parenting for Peace and Justice*. Rev. ed. Maryknoll, N.Y.: Orbis Books, 1990.

May, Elaine Tyler. *Homeward Bound: American Families in the Cold War*. New York: Basic Books, 1988.

Merton, Thomas. *Zen and the Birds of Appetite*. New York: New Directions, 1968.

Miller, Alice. *For Your Own Good: Hidden Cruelty in Child-rearing and the Roots of Violence*. New York: Farrar, Straus and Giroux, 1984.

Miller, Jean Baker. *Toward a New Psychology of Women*. 2d ed. Boston: Beacon Press, 1986.

Mische, Gerald, and Patricia Mische. *Toward a Human World Order: Beyond the National Security Straitjacket.* New York: Paulist Press, 1977.

Musto, Ronald G. *The Catholic Peace Tradition.* Maryknoll, N.Y.: Orbis Books, 1986.

Myers, Norman, ed. *Gaia: An Atlas of Planet Management.* Garden City, N.Y.: Anchor Press/Doubleday, 1984.

Nelson, Jack B. *The Intimate Connection: Male Sexuality, Masculine Spirituality.* Philadelphia: Westminster Press, 1988.

O'Connor, Flannery. *Three by Flannery O'Connor.* New York: New American Library, 1962.

Orwell, George. "Politics and the English Language." In *A Collection of Essays.* New York: Harbrace Paperback Library, 1954.

Person, Ethel Spector. *Dreams of Love and Fateful Encounters: The Power of Romantic Passion.* New York: W. W. Norton and Co., 1988.

Pruett, Kyle D. *The Nurturing Father: Journey toward the Complete Man.* New York: Warner Books, 1987.

Rossi, Alice S. "The Biosocial Side of Parenthood." in Dorothy Rogers, ed., *Issues in Life-span Human Development.* Monterey, Calif.: Brooks/Cole Publishing Co., 1980.

Sagan, Carl, and Ann Druyan. "An Open Letter to the New President—For the Sake of Our Children's Future . . . Give Us Hope." *Parade: The Sunday Newspaper Magazine,* November 27, 1988.

Singer, Jerome L., and Dorothy G. Singer. *Television, Imagination, and Aggression: A Study of Preschoolers.* Hillsdale, N.J.: Lawrence Erlbaum Associates, 1981.

Smith, Sam. "Twelve Ways To Make It through the Bush Era: A Survival Guide." *Utne Reader* (November-December 1989): 110–11.

Smith, Wilfred Cantwell. *The Meaning and End of Religion.* New York: Harper and Row, 1962.

Soldi, Anna. "A Heart Made of Bread." *Global Perspectives: A Quarterly Newsletter of the Center for Global Education at Augsburg College* (Winter 1988): Write: 721 21st Ave. So., Minneapolis, Minn. 55454. 6–7, 11.

Spier, Peter. *People.* New York: Doubleday and Co., 1980.

Spock, Benjamin. *Dr. Spock on Parenting.* New York: Pocket Books, 1988.

Thomas, Daniel C., and Michael T. Klare, eds. *Peace and World Order Studies: A Curriculum Guide,* 5th ed. Boulder, Colo.: Westview Press, 1989.

True, Michael. *Homemade Social Justice: Teaching Peace and Justice in the Home.* Mystic, Conn.: Twenty-Third Publications, 1982.

———. *Justice-seekers, Peacemakers: 32 Portraits in Courage.* Mystic, Conn.: Twenty-Third Publications, 1985.

Vanderhaar, Gerard A. *Enemies and How To Love Them.* Mystic, Conn.: Twenty-Third Publications, 1985.

Vidal, Gore. *Matters of Fact and of Fiction: Essays 1973–1976.* New York: Random House, 1977.

Westley, Dick. *Morality and Its Beyond.* Mystic, Conn.: Twenty-Third Publications, 1984.

Withorn, Ann. *Serving the People: Social Service and Social Change.* New York: Columbia University Press, 1984.

Witvliet, Theo. *A Place in the Sun: An Introduction to Liberation Theology in the Third World.* Maryknoll, N.Y.: Orbis Books, 1984.

Zinn, Howard. *Disobedience and Democracy: Nine Fallacies on Law and Order.* New York: Random House, 1968.